PAINLESS PRESENTATIONS

The Proven, Stress-Free Way to Successful Public Speaking

LENNY LASKOWSKI

WILEY

John Wiley & Sons, Inc.

Published by John Wiley & Sons, Inc., Hoboken, New Jersey.
Published simultaneously in Canada.

For general information on our other products and services or technical support, please contact our Customer Care Department within the United States at (800) 762-2974, outside the United States at (317) 572-3993 or fax (317) 572-4002.

Wiley publishes in a variety of print and electronic formats and by print-on-demand. Some material included with standard print versions of this book may not be included in e-books or in print-on-demand. If this book refers to media such as a CD or DVD that is not included in the version you purchased, you may download this material at http://booksupport.wiley.com. For more information about wiley products, visit www.wiley.com.

ISBN 978-1-118-36177-1 (paper); ISBN 978-1-118-43146-7 (ebk);
ISBN 978-1-118-43149-8 (ebk); ISBN 978-1-118-43150-4 (ebk)

Printed in the United States of America

10 9 8 7 6 5 4 3 2 1

Contents

CONTENTS

CHAPTER 1

The Seven Aspects of Speaking

Delivering a presentation is one of the greatest fears of many people. It does not matter if you are a business professional, a student, a member of the cloth, a teacher, or a politician—preparing and delivering a presentation can be a painful process. Being asked to deliver a presentation brings back bad memories from our early school years when we had to deliver our first oral book report. Many of us were told to pick a book, read it, and prepare an oral book report without being given any guidance. We had no structure or idea how to prepare for this life-changing event.

That event was one of the most frightening events in many people's lives, and many of you probably still remember the sweaty palms, the nervousness, and the butterflies in your stomach. That fear, more commonly known as speaking anxiety, can stay with you an entire lifetime, unless you are taught how to overcome these fears. *Painless Presentations: The Proven Stress-Free Way to Successful Public Speaking* provides the tools and techniques to help you learn how to reduce your speaking anxiety and deliver a more stress-free presentation.

To be a successful speaker, one needs to learn and understand many aspects of a presentation. This chapter will discuss these seven aspects. An effective speaker learns to deal with all these aspects at the same time. The seven aspects are as follows:

Aspect 1—The Speaker

Aspect 2—The Message

Aspect 3—The Audience

Aspect 4—The Channel

Aspect 5—The Feedback

Aspect 6—The Noise

Aspect 7—The Setting

The following pages discuss these important aspects and how they relate to making an effective presentation.

ASPECT 1—THE SPEAKER

One of the key components of the act of public speaking is the speaker, the source of the message. Several factors should be addressed about any speaker. As a speaker, you need to understand what your motivation is in giving your presentation. Is your motivation to inform people? Is your motivation to convince people? Is your motivation unclear to you?

Your Motivation

Before you develop and deliver your presentation, you need to understand what motivates you. At least two factors affect your motivation:

- Are you motivated by *direct* personal rewards (e.g., money) or *indirect* rewards (e.g., feeling good about helping others)?
- Are you motivated by *immediate* rewards (e.g., money today) or *delayed* rewards (e.g., establishing a broader client base by professional exposure)?

The most important motivation of all is to teach, help, and inspire your audience. You will not become a great speaker unless you are motivated.

Your Credibility

Your ideas are accepted only to the degree that you are perceived as being credible. Your credibility rests on your trustworthiness, your competence, and your goodwill. You need to be well organized to be considered credible.

It is a known fact that a speaker who is attractive and dynamic will be perceived as more credible than a speaker who is undistinguished and dull.

The most fundamental attitude you can project is a true caring for your audience. Your audience needs to believe you really care about them.

Your Delivery

Your delivery, the *way* your message is presented, should complement your presentation or speech's objective. It is often said, "It's not *what* you said, but *how* you said it." A poorly delivered presentation can be the result of many factors. Unfortunately, many presenters do not practice their delivery prior to the actual presentation. If you practice delivering your presentation at least once, you will be doing more than 80 percent of most presenters today.

When you practice your delivery, you should always record yourself so that you can later watch it. There is no excuse for anyone not having the ability to record his or her presentation. Video cameras today are very small, easy to use, and inexpensive. In addition to digital movie cameras, there are also video recording options available on Flip cameras, smartphones, and digital cameras. It is in your best interest to use these tools to help you improve your presentations.

ASPECT 2—THE MESSAGE

The message is found in *everything you say or do*—in other words, in all that is communicated, both verbally and nonverbally. The verbal component of your presentation can be analyzed in terms of three basic elements:

1. The content of your message
2. Your speaking style
3. The structure of your presentation

Let's take a look at each of these elements.

The Content of Your Message

The content is what you say about your topic. The content is the meat of your speech or presentation. When developing the content for your presentation, you need to research the topic very thoroughly. Collect as much information as you can during your preparation. Gather more material than you think you may need.

Your next step is to decide how much to say about every point of information. It is critical that your presentation not only have content but also provide value. You need to consider your audience's needs, time factors, and other variable as you prepare and present the content of your presentation.

All great speakers have a great topic, one they have lived. They are what buyers call real people. A speech or presentation based on research only is never a great one. A speech or presentation based on actual experience is always more effective. Great speakers learn to use stories to help their audiences experience what they experienced.

Before you begin to develop your presentation, you need to decide what message you want to convey to your audience. Most presentations fail because the message is unclear. Your intended message may not agree with the message your audience received.

When this occurs, then your presentation can fail. You need to decide what message you want to deliver, determine what you want your audience to do as a result of hearing this message, and then build your presentation around this message. This is a crucial step in the process that many presenters do not do effectively. Once you align your presentation with your message, your presentations will be easier to develop and deliver.

Your Speaking Style

The manner in which you present the content of your presentation is your speaking style. Speaking styles can range from the very formal to the very informal. Your presentation style should fall somewhere in between these extremes and in every case should be determined by what is appropriate to you, your audience, and the setting. Every speaker has his or her own style, and you should develop your own personal style. Many beginning speakers try to emulate other speakers. I do not recommend this. Learn to develop your own personal speaking style.

Regardless of your experience with presentations, the real key to delivering an effective presentation is to approach them using a conversational style. Unfortunately many people approach presentations as a performance. When you are in performance mode, you typically are focusing on what your audience is thinking and not on what you are saying. The good news is you already have years of experience having a conversation with people. You do this every single day. Think about it.

When you run into someone you know, whether it is at your favorite restaurant, the grocery store, or a meeting where you are not the speaker, you typically just strike up a conversation. After you greet each other, you conversationally talk about work, your family, and how things are going. While having this conversation, you are not thinking about what you are doing with your hands, what words you are saying, or even how you are speaking. You just have a conversation. It is this same conversational style you want to use when you give a presentation.

Many of my clients and participants in my seminars and workshops often ask me, "What is the difference between a formal presentation and one that is not?" Some people think that as soon as you stand up in front of a group of people, the presentation is formal. The key to being a more effective presenter and making it less painful to you is to learn to simply have a conversation with your audience. This will allow you to connect with them more effectively. Use your own natural conversational style, and you will find that your presentations will be not only easier for you to deliver but more enjoyable as well.

The Structure of Your Presentation

The structure of your presentation is its organization. There are many variations with how you can organize your presentation, but in every case, your presentation's structure should include three major components:

- Introduction
- Body
- Conclusion

The first part of every presentation is the introduction. The introduction is where you tell or introduce what you will be talking about during your presentation. The introduction provides an outline of your presentation. You typically spend only about 10 to 15 percent of your presentation time with the introduction.

The middle part of your presentation is the body. The body is where you discuss your key points or main ideas. The body is where the "meat" of your presentation and key message are discussed. This part of the presentation is where you will spend the majority of your time, typically about 70 to 80 percent of the time.

The last part of your presentation is the conclusion. The conclusion is where you conclude your presentation by summarizing the key points you made during the body of your presentation. You typically spend only about 10 to 15 percent of your presentation time with the conclusion.

When your presentation is poorly organized, the impact of your message is greatly reduced and your audience is less likely to accept you or your ideas. Chapter 3 will discuss the structure of a presentation in greater detail and what should be included in each section.

ASPECT 3—THE AUDIENCE

A key part of any presentation is the audience. A great presentation delivered to the wrong audience is just as ineffective as delivering the wrong presentation to the right audience. Both will fail terribly. As a presenter you must include some detailed analysis about the audience you will be speaking to as part of your preparation.

Professional speakers, such as myself, always take the time to gather as much information as possible about the audience we will be speaking to before we start customizing our material. It is not unusual for me to make several phone calls and even have an in-person meeting with the meeting planner or the actual client who has hired me to discuss the expected outcomes and desire of the meeting. As a professional speaker, you would always analyze your audience and determine their specific needs and objectives.

This will allow you to prepare and give the most effective, meaningful, and memorable presentation to your audience.

The analysis you perform should include considerations related to:

- Age
- Sex
- Marital status
- Race
- Geographic location
- Group memberships
- Education
- Career

For example, if you are preparing a presentation on "future careers," knowing your audience's average age is vital. All audiences you speak to want to know:

1. You will not waste their time.
2. You know who they are.
3. You are well organized.
4. You know your subject.
5. You will be clear about your most important point.
6. You will be clear when you are finished.

Your speech preparation should include what I like to refer to as the nine Ps:

Prior Proper Preparation Prevents Poor Performance of the **Person Putting** on the **Presentation.**

Nothing will relax you more than knowing you are properly prepared. The more you know about your speaking environment and your audience, the more relaxed you will be when delivering your presentation.

There are two parts of performing an audience analysis: the pre-program survey and the customized program survey. Both address the areas described here, which spell of the acronym *AUDIENCE*. You need to develop specific questions that fit into each of these eight categories and ask your audience what they want. Ask them what they want and then give it to them.

- *Analysis:* Who is your audience? How many people will be in your audience?
- *Understanding:* What is their knowledge of your topic or subject on which you plan to speak?
- *Demographics:* Where is your audience from? What is their age? What is their sex? What is their background?
- *Interest:* Why is your audience there? Why are they attending? Were they told to be at this event, or are they there on their own accord?
- *Environment:* Where will you be standing during your presentation? Will everyone be able to see you during your presentation? Will they be able to hear you?
- *Needs:* What are the needs of your audience? Why are they here to listen to this presentation topic? What are your needs as a presenter?
- *Customize:* Do some homework to customize your presentation. What information do you need to address in your presentation to meet your audience's needs?
- *Expectations:* What are your expectations of this presentation? What is the expectation of your audience?

On the next few pages, I will offer you some suggestions of the types of pre-program questions you could ask about your audience. You can provide these survey questions to them by mail, by fax, over the phone, or via a web survey. I currently use SurveyMonkey (www.surveymonkey.com) for my customized pre-program surveys. This tool allows me to easily collect the information I need in advance, and it is presented to me in several formats. This is a very cool tool that allows me to gather as much information as I want about my audience.

Following is an example pre-program survey I send out to learn additional information about my audience. Feel free to use these questions or make up a survey of your own based on your specific needs. I recommend that you send this survey out well in advance of your speaking date. Also be prepared to follow up and gently remind people to complete the surveys. Give them a drop-dead date of when you need the completed surveys.

What You Need to Know (Pre-Program Survey)

1. What are your organization's major needs, problems, and concerns at this moment?

2. How much do your members know about the subject of my presentation?

3. What is their level of knowledge about the topic? Do they have some knowledge, have very little knowledge, or consider themselves as an expert on the topic?

4. What is their level of education?

5. How large will the audience be?

6. What is the ratio of men to women who will be attending?

7. What are the occupations of this audience?

8. What is the main purpose of this meeting? Is there a theme for the meeting?

9. Are there any sensitive political issues I need to be aware of?

10. Are there any sensitive religious issues I need to be aware of?

11. Will there be any other speakers on the program before me or after me?

12. Will there be eating and drinking before my presentation?

13. Have you had presenters in the past speak on this topic or a similar topic?

14. If so, what has been the audience's reaction to this topic?

15. What type of information or supportive information may I need?

The answers to these questions will help you better understand your audience and their expectations. The more you can find out about your audience, the better you will be able to address their needs.

A Customized Program Survey

You can always provide a more in-depth pre-program survey customized to your speaking event. Once you and the client have agreed on the topic you will speak on, ask your contact at the client if he or she would provide you answers to your customized survey. Some of the customized program survey questions are similar to the pre-program survey questions and that's by design.

1. What is the theme of your meeting?

2. What are the top three challenges or problems faced by the members of your group?

3. What are the characteristics of your typical member?
   a. Age
   b. Sex
   c. Personal income
   d. Educational background
   e. Occupation
4. Will there be any special guests?
5. How many people will be in attendance?
6. How will they be notified about the meeting?
7. What is their overall opinion regarding this subject?
8. What three factors should I know about your group before I speak to them?
9. Why is your group attending this meeting?
10. What speakers have you booked recently, and what topics did they discuss?
11. What programs/speakers have been the most enthusiastically received?
12. List three names and positions of people in your organization who are well known and well liked?
13. What are the three most significant events during the past year?
14. Please share any "local color" you can think of relating to the location at which my presentation will be held.
15. Specifically, what are you trying to accomplish at this meeting?
16. What are your specific objectives for my part of the meeting?
17. Are there any issues/topics you think I should discuss during my program?

18. Are there any issues/topics you think I should avoid during the program?

19. Do you have any suggestions to help me make this presentation the best your audience had ever heard?

Remember, the information you gather from the pre-program survey will help you customize and tailor your presentation to the specific audience. The actual questions you ask as part of your program preparation should be specific to the program you are providing and the specific group to whom you will be speaking. The more information you can gather about your audience, the better it will be for you and the easier it will be to tailor your program.

As part of my preparation, I like to do some research on the client who has hired me to speak. This may include reading reports on the company website, press releases, or even an article I found in a newspaper. I sometimes will even contact other professional speakers who have spoken to the group to gain additional insight from another professional speaker's viewpoint. You can never gather too much information as part of your preparation.

I also always try to arrive early to the venue. This may be during the evening before my presentation, or it may be a few hours before I speak. This gives me the opportunity to speak to the actual people who will be in the audience. This allows me to gather some names and some "on the spot" expectations for my presentation. When I can, I will incorporate the conversations I had in my presentation and mention the names of the people I spoke with. This allows me to gain a better connection with the audience.

When I am facilitating a seminar or workshop, I am always the first one to arrive because I need to set up the room and the equipment. (I will talk about the room setting when I get to Aspect 7—The Setting.) I greet the attendees as they enter the room. By doing this, I am able to establish an immediate rapport and connection with the participants in my seminars and workshops. Greeting them also demonstrates that I am accessible and approachable.

The Size of the Audience

One factor that can greatly influence your presentation is the size of the audience. You need to take the audience size into consideration as part of your preparation. Delivering the same presentation to an audience of 100 people is a lot different than delivering the same presentation to a group of more than 6,000. I have personally spoken to groups as large as 14,000. For large groups, I am generally on a large stage with two large screens, one on either side of me, while a large spotlight shines directly in my eyes, not allowing me to see much of the audience. Knowing the size of the venue and the number of people I will be speaking to greatly influences how I prepare for this presentation.

ASPECT 4—THE CHANNEL

When you communicate during a presentation, you use several communication channels to convey your message. When you talk directly to an audience, you will employ many different types of communication channels, such as:

A. Nonverbal
   1. Gestures
   2. Facial expressions
   3. Body movement
   4. Posture

B. Pictorial

   1. Diagrams

   2. Charts

   3. Graphs

   4. Pictures

   5. Objects

C. Aural

   1. Tones of voice

   2. Variations in pitch and volume

   3. Other vocal variety

Let's look at each of these in more depth. Most of our communication occurs on the nonverbal level. Nonverbal communication is that communication you use other than the words you are speaking. Most of your nonverbal communication is provided through the use of gestures, facial expressions, body movement, and posture. When your verbal and nonverbal messages do not agree, you can send a mixed or even confusing message to your audience. We have all experienced this. You have heard the expression, "Actions speak louder than words." Or maybe someone has said to you, "It's not what you said, but how you said it." As a presenter, you need be sure your verbal and nonverbal messages are in alignment with each other; otherwise, you can send a mixed message.

Our body movement is the largest single gesture or nonverbal message we can use. If you do not use your body movement effectively, you can confuse your audience, preventing them from understanding what you are saying. I will discuss this in greater detail in Chapter 6 on nonverbal messages.

Our second major communication channel is pictorial. This refers to the types of visual aids you use during your presentations. They can include diagrams, charts, graphs, pictures or photographs, or physical objects. Just as with nonverbal communication, you need to be sure the pictorial communication tools you use during your presentation align with your verbal message. For example, if the photograph you are showing is not about what you are talking about, the audience will get confused. You want your visual aid to enhance your presentation and further support or clarify your message.

The last communication channel is aural, that is, your voice. How your voices sounds, the variations in your pitch and volume, can have a huge effect on the meaning of your words. The tone of your voice is what can persuade someone or get you in trouble. Has your significant other ever said to you, "It's not what you said, but how you said it"? Or maybe, "I don't like the tone of your voice"? When you get emotional during your presentation, this will be reflected in the tone of your voice.

Most messages are sent via light waves and sound waves and are received by the eyes and ears. The more sensory channels a speaker can use at the same time, the more effective the presentation will be. At the same time, if the various channels used are not in alignment, you will confuse or even upset your audience.

ASPECT 5—THE FEEDBACK

This next aspect deals with the subject of feedback. By *feedback*, I mean the process through which you receive information about how your message is being received by the listeners in your audience, and in turn, responding to those cues.

The feedback process is not complete until you have responded to your listener. This feedback process also includes the audience's reaction to your response. As a presenter, you need to be alert and responsive to the reactions of your audience throughout your entire presentation. Watch for nonverbal clues from your audience and be prepared to respond to their reactions. You can also ask questions of the audience during your presentation to get them more engaged. Ask them what their understanding is of a point you have just made.

It is your responsibility to provide the information your audience needs to hear. Many times, I am hired by a client to speak to the staff and provide a specific message they may not want to hear. Recently I was hired to address an entire national sales force of a company during one of my sales presentation skills programs. During this 90-minute presentation, I discussed many issues on how to increase their sales and improve their relationships with their clients. As part of my preparation for this presentation, I had several meetings, phone calls, and e-mails with the owner of the business, who hired me to speak to this staff. We talked about problems he was aware of with his staff's sales presentations and a number of other issues. Before my arrival, I knew, by name, which people were the top salespeople as well as which ones were not meeting expectations. I also learned what specific problems and challenges they faced. I also learned about past presenters the company had brought in and how the staff treated and reacted to those speakers. Knowing a lot about this audience allowed me to develop a customized, issue-focused presentation that addressed the problems they were experiencing, including providing solutions to these problems. I learned as much information as I could about the company and the sale forces so that I was prepared to address any questions that may have come up.

I was able to interact with the audience by addressing people by their first name, further allowing me to establish a better rapport with the audience. I was able to also use their industry's jargon and language as well as include specifics about their company. Many of the salespeople came up to me after the presentation and said how they appreciated how much I truly understood their business and their challenges. I knew then that I hit a home run.

ASPECT 6—THE NOISE

There are two types of noise you need to deal with as a presenter: external noise and internal noise. Both types of noise can greatly affect your presentation. Let's look at each.

External Noise

External noise for presenters includes those sounds from the external environment that can distract them during their presentation. External noise includes sounds, temperature (either cold or hot), announcements over an intercom, people talking or laughing, audience movement, poor seating arrangement, poor lighting, or even an obstructed view. Let me share some real-life examples I have personally had to deal with my speaking career.

Temperature

As a professional speaker, I have had to present in a room as cold as 50 degrees. I was conducting a two-day seminar in Dayton, Ohio, for a client in late October. The two-day seminar was being held in the client's conference room, which was part of their rented office space. I asked why it was so cold in the building and why the heat was not on. The client told me that the owner of the office building did not turn on the heat to the building until November 1. This was a situation that made both me and the participants in my program physically uncomfortable. The cold temperature made it very difficult for anyone to concentrate.

On another occasion, I was providing four days of training at a hotel in Dubai, UAE. The air-conditioning in the building was not working properly, and the room we were in for all four days was about 85 degrees. With outside temperatures well over 100 degrees, we did not have many options. This too was very uncomfortable for both me and my audience.

Too Many External Distractions

A number of years ago, I was delivering a short 90-minute program in San Francisco at the Moscone Center. The Moscone Center is the largest convention center and exhibition complex in San Francisco, California. This convention had more than 20,000 attendees, and I was one of more than 100 speakers presenting during the week of this convention. This had to be the worst speaking setup I ever had to deal with as a speaker. I was speaking from a large stage in the center of the complex. The microphone provided for me worked very well; however, so did the other two microphones that were being used by two other speakers also speaking at the same time within this same complex. My audience included more than 500 people who were seated at tables in a large open area. There were no walls, and I had to compete with the background noise from the convention activities as well as the other two speakers. My audience had to sit at a bank of tables much like you sit at in a college classroom. On these tables were also banks of computers. You can imagine the challenge I had to keep the attention of my audience. I had no ability to make any changes in this setup. When I was invited back to speak to this same group at the same convention center the following year, I politely declined.

As a presenter, you never know what variety of external noise you may have to deal with. Your goal is to eliminate or at least reduce the amount of external distraction that you can, within the limitations of your control.

Obstructed View

I was hired to provide a workshop for another client in the basement of a church. This was a very large church hall that was frequently used for special events. The seats were arranged in auditorium-style seating (I will talk more about seating when I talk about the setting). The seating was set up for about 200 people. Like many church basements, square columns were spaced 10 feet apart in several directions. More than a dozen of these square poles were scattered among the 200 seats. Fortunately, I had checked this room out beforehand, so I was aware of the room setup. I knew I needed to make some adjustments during my presentation. Specifically, I had to make a point to conscientiously move during my entire presentation in order to establish eye contact with the members of my audience. I also had to move to allow the audience to see me. Because I had checked out the room beforehand and was able to make adjustments in my delivery, I was able to deal with these square columns.

Talking to an Audience Who Does Not Speak Your Language

My business has allowed me to establish a client base in more than 178 countries, and I often find myself speaking to audiences whose first language is not English. I speak only English. I provide several multiday programs each year to clients in the Middle East. The programs I provide are marketed and delivered in both English and Arabic. Since I speak only English, I have an interpreter who translates what I say and repeats what I say in Arabic for those who do not understand English. Pulling off the logistics and planning to allow my presentation to be delivered in both English and Arabic was no easy task.

The interpreters I used in all the programs I have provided have all been women. These interpreters had to spend time learning not only my program but my speaking style. I also had to learn to adjust the delivery of my presentation in more bite-size sound bites to allow my interpreter to repeat what I said, but in Arabic. The slides I used for my presentation were also in English and Arabic. I provide several programs each year and typically have participants from more than 22 Arabic countries for this three-day program. You can imagine the extent of external distractions that can occur during a program such as this.

■ ■ ■

The examples just described are only a few examples I had to personally deal with during my professional speaking career. As a speaker, you too will have to deal with external distractions. How you deal with these distractions can be and will be a challenge to you as a presenter.

Internal Noise

As a presenter you may encounter internal noise in two forms: personal internal noise and audience internal noise. If you are confused or unclear about what you want to express, it is because you do not know or have misanalyzed the audience, resulting in internal voices of doubt and panic. You also need to account for the internal noise directly experienced by the audience. Such internal noise may result from one of many stressors, such as fatigue, job insecurity, rapid changes in the workplace, and family concerns. The role of both you and the audience is to communicate simultaneously with each other. It is this transactional nature of speech that makes feedback, and attempts to decrease or eliminate noise, so vitally important.

The most effective ways you can combat noise are:

- Use more than one channel of communication at the same time (verbal and nonverbal).
- Use repetition and restatement.

You can further help combat noise by making an extra effort to use several channels of communication at the same time. It is important to include both verbal and nonverbal means of communication. You can also lessen the effects of noise by giving listeners more than one chance to hear the message, thus the need for repetition and restatement.

Speaking Anxiety

The one internal source of noise or distraction important enough to be treated by itself is stage fright or speaking anxiety. Steve Allen, a television personality, musician, and past host of the *Steve Allen Show* and the *Tonight Show* for many years, said, "Stage fright does not begin when you get up on stage; stage fright begins the moment that you are asked to get up on stage."

Inexperienced presenters, and to some degree even experienced presenters, feel stress in anticipation of speaking in public. Presenters with high anxiety may report symptoms such as butterflies in their stomach, increased heart rate, trembling legs, and cold clammy hands, among many other symptoms. You decide how you label these feelings. Are they stage fright or speech anxiety? Or are they speech excitement? What you choose to call them has a noticeable effect on whether you control them or they control you.

There have been several informal studies done over the years, including survey studies I have done with a variety of speaker types over the past 20 years reviewing the anxiety levels associated with the degree of speaking experience. My data were collected from surveying more than 17,000 speakers, ranging from college students to executives and the results are summarized in Figure 1.1.

Referring to Figure 1.1 let me explain to you what the collected survey data show. This figure represents a plot of speaker anxiety levels over time for four speaker types.

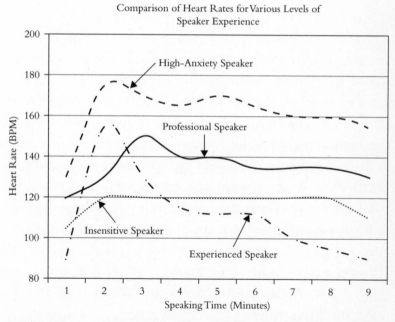

Figure 1.1 Comparison of high-anxiety speakers, experienced speakers, insensitive speakers, and professional speakers.

- High-anxiety speaker
- Experienced speaker
- Insensitive speaker
- Professional speaker

The level of speaking anxiety was measured by the speaker's heart rate over the course of about eight minutes' speaking time. On the y-axis I have plotted the average heart rates, measured in beats per minute (BPM). Along the x-axis I have plotted speaking time measured in minutes. Keep in mind that a typical normal heart rate is around 70 BPM.

Let's first examine the plot for the high-anxiety speaker. The high-anxiety speaker's heart rate starts off at around 130 BPM and quickly rises to about 175 BPM. Many famous actors and actresses have high anxiety when speaking in front of a group. I have read stories that Johnny Carson, the host of the *Tonight Show*, had a heart rate so high in the beginning of his show that during his opening monologue, he had to wear a heart monitor so that they could monitor how high his heart rate got. As you follow the plot for the high-anxiety speaker, you notice that the heart rate does not reduce that much, even after eight minutes of speaking.

Next let's look at the experienced speaker. This is a speaker who has a lot of speaking experience but who cannot optimally control his or her anxiety throughout the presentation. Note that this speaker's heart rate starts off lower, at around 90 BPM, and then rises, but only to about 155 BPM. The profile soon fades off back to the 90 BPM toward the end of the eight minutes' speaking time.

Next we look at the insensitive speaker. This is the speaker who really can care less during the presentation. This speaker gets up, delivers the presentation, and quickly sits down. He or she is very flat and boring in facial expressions and not very exciting to listen to. This behavior is reflected in the plot on the graph. The plot remains flat during the entire presentation, showing no real response or emotional reaction to the audience.

Finally we look at the professional speaker. The professional speaker is one who understands how to use this nervous energy to his or her advantage. These speakers allow their heart rates to be elevated to about 120 BPM (a good aerobic range) before they begin speaking. Some speakers go for a brisk walk, some exercise, and others just let the heart rate slowly increase. Their heart rates do also increase, but not as quickly and only to a level around 150 BPM. Over the remaining time, they maintain an elevated heart rate (or excitement) around 130 BPM. This is the type speaker who continues to show enthusiasm and passion throughout the presentation but also does not let it get out of control. You have to make a conscious effort to keep your heart rate elevated, and this is usually done through personal excitement and passion while speaking.

In all cases, there was an elevation in the heart rate within the first few minutes of speaking; however, how that level changed over time varied greatly. As a presenter, you do want to have some anxiety before you speak; however, you do not want an anxiety level so high that your heart races too fast and you find yourself out of breath. Just knowing that this peak does occur and learning what you need to do to get through it will be key.

This elevated heart rate is the same increase in heart rate we experience when falling in love with someone for the first time; however, you probably associate this feeling as a "good" feeling and work your way through it. Whether your heart rate increases due to speaking anxiety or being in love, the physiological feelings that your body experiences are the same.

Some of the other classic symptoms associated with this speaking anxiety are:

- Accelerated or increased heart rate
- Trembling or shaky hands
- Sweaty palms
- Difficulty in breathing
- Tingling or numbness in our hand and fingers
- Nausea or stomach sickness
- Chest pains
- Shaky voice
- Dry mouth or cotton mouth
- Dizziness
- Feeling of choking
- Hot or cold flashes

Most people with speaking anxiety experience one or more of these symptoms. These feelings often originate when the speaker is approaching public speaking or giving a presentation as if it is a performance, sometime referred to as performance anxiety. When you put yourself in "performance mode," you imagine everyone is looking at you differently and analyzing and scrutinizing every move you make and every word you say. When in this performance mode, you start to think too much about what you are saying and how you are saying it, while at the same time worrying about what the audience is thinking. You are thinking about everything except what you should be thinking about—your message.

When you find yourself in this state of performance mode, mentally stop and go back to your message. Try to focus on just having a conversation. Think about it: when you run into a friend in the store and kick up a conversation, do you think to yourself or say to yourself, "I wonder what he is thinking about me. Do I sound okay?" No you don't; you just have a conversation. As a professional speaker, I travel all over the world and I always get asked the same question: "What is the one piece of advice you can tell me to help me with my speaking anxiety?" I always respond with the same answer: "Just learn to have a conversation." We all know how to do that. We all have conversations every single day. Notice how you converse with people and bring that same conversational style to the stage when you are delivering a presentation. Deliver that presentation using your natural conversational style, and you will find your anxiety will greatly reduce. Notice I said reduce, not go away.

As I explained earlier when I described the different types of speakers, you want that slightly increased heart rate. When you start to use conversational-style speaking, you also naturally use gestures more effectively without even thinking about what you are doing with your hands. Try this: the next time you are out and about, find a couple or even a group of people talking and you will notice that they are using natural gestures. They are using their hands, nodding their heads, even moving their bodies. They are not giving a presentation, but just having a conversation—but, a conversation with energy, passion, and excitement. During your next presentation, just try having a conversation with the audience. You will be amazed how much better you will feel.

Following are some additional things you can do to prepare yourself for your next presentation. Many of these deal with some of the aspects I have already talked about.

1. *Know the room.* Arrive at the event location early to become familiar with the space where you will be speaking. Is it on a stage, on the floor at the same level as the audience, or behind a lectern (which I personally never use and encourage you not to use)? Walk around the room, stand at the lectern, get up on stage, look out at the empty chairs, and test your microphone. Get a "feeling" for the environment you will be speaking in. *Note:* Be sure you are doing this in the actual room you will be speaking in, which is something you should confirm beforehand. If you will be speaking on a podium (a raised platform), check out the podium to make sure it is secure and stable. Notice where the ends of the podium are. I often put some tape on the edges of the podium if it is not already taped. This provides me with a visual of where the podium ends. If you are a woman and wearing high heels, check to make sure there are no gaps large enough in the podium floor that can catch the heal of your shoe and cause you to trip or, worse, fall. Have these gaps taped if necessary. Walk up and down the stairs to get a feel of how high the steps are. Sometimes they are higher than your average steps, which could throw you off when you walk up on stage. Do not wait to be introduced to test these stairs.

2. *Know your audience.* If possible, arrive early and personally greet some members of the audience as they arrive and chat with them. If the event you are speaking at has a social hour the evening before, attend and introduce yourself; get to know some of the people by first name. You may even be able to use some of the information obtained from these conversations during your presentation. When you are on

stage presenting and having a conversation with the audience, mention some of these people by name. This will help you better connect with members in the audience.

3. *Know your material.* If you are not familiar with or are uncomfortable with your material, your nervousness will escalate. You need to rehearse your presentation several times to be comfortable with your material. You will find when you rehearse that the wording you used in your notes does not work well when spoken and that you need to say things differently. In every one of my presentation skills workshops I require each of the participants to do a rehearsal (dry run) while standing and talking in the location where they will be delivering their final presentations (they will do this several times during my workshops). In every case, when I ask each person if he or she would make any changes in the presentation after this first dry run, the answer is always yes. The speakers find that what came out their mouths was not what was going on in their heads. This is why I strongly encourage you to always use conversational language in your presentations. This includes using conversational language in your visual aids. If you decide to write out (for planning purposes) in general terms what you want to say, write it down using conversational language and phrasing. Many of us do not write like we speak and do not speak like we write. The more we learn to write like we speak, the easier the speaking process becomes. This reminds me of a time when I was having a beer in the lounge of the hotel where I was scheduled to do the opening keynote the next day. I noticed a gentleman sitting at a table frantically typing away on his laptop

computer. I looked over his shoulder and noticed he was preparing some PowerPoint slides. I walked over to him and introduced myself and asked him what he was doing. He said he was scheduled to give a presentation tomorrow but had not had a chance to prepare his slides for the presentation. I asked him why he waited until the last minute to do this, and he said, and I quote, "I do not like giving presentations. I suck at it, and I find it is better to wait until the last minute." I could not believe what I heard, so I asked him why he thought it was better to wait until the last minute. He replied, "I don't know why, but I am always so nervous when I have to present and put it off until last minute." How many of you have done exactly what this guy did?

4. *Relax*. You can ease any tension and anxiety you have by doing some exercises just before your presentation. Sit comfortably back in a chair with your back straight. Breathe in slowly, hold your breath for four to five seconds, and slowly exhale. Repeat this several times. Find a quiet spot where you can walk around and loosen up your leg muscles. Shake your hands and get your blood circulating more in your hands and feet. Do some type of physical warm-up routine to reestablish your blood flow in your hands, feet and your head.

Let me digress a little here and explain to you why this is important. Earlier I talked about the symptoms of speaking anxiety. I need to explain to you exactly what is going on physiologically in your body. Let's start with the accelerated heart rate. What is the function of your heart? The function of your heart is to pump blood to all parts of your body. What is the function of your blood? The function of your blood is to carry oxygen to the various parts of your body. When your heart beats fast, it is pumping blood much quicker into and out of the heart because it needs more oxygen. Your body has a finite amount of blood, and when your heart beats much faster than normal, the blood it needs is drawn into your heart away from the extremities of your body. This includes your hands, feet, and even your head. As this occurs, your hands and feet may start to "tingle." When you notice this "tingling," you say to yourself, "Oh my God, I must be getting nervous." And what happens . . . your heart beats faster and before long your body spirals out of control. As you begin to notice and feel more symptoms and your knees begin to shake, and as the other parts of your body begin to react, you find yourself out of control. You then say to yourself, "See, I knew I would get nervous."

To get this under control you need to use some techniques, which I will be discussing very soon in the next section.

5. *Visualize yourself speaking.* Imagine yourself walking confidently to the lectern as the audience is applauding. Imagine yourself speaking. Listen to yourself projecting your voice in a clear and assured manner. When you visualize yourself being successful, you will be successful. Unfortunately, many people visualize themselves failing, making a fool of themselves. It is often said, "If you think you will succeed you will. If you think you will fail, you will." You decide which belief you prefer. Visualization is a very, very powerful tool used by many successful speakers, athletes, and actors. Start visualizing yourself being successful.

6. *Realize that people want you to succeed.* All audiences want presenters to be interesting, stimulating, and entertaining. They *want* you to succeed. When was the last time you went to hear a presenter and you said to yourself, "Boy I hope this presenter is the worst presenter I ever heard"? Then why do we think our audiences are going to want us to be bad presenters. They don't! Too many nervous presenters are their own worst enemy. They imagine that the audience will not like them, creating all kinds of reasons why. WRONG! You audience wants you to succeed.

7. *Don't apologize.* Most of the time your nervousness does not show at all. Many of the participants in my workshops are amazed when they watch their videos of them speaking that they do not look nervous, even though they remember being nervous. Seeing themselves and knowing how they felt is very powerful. Powerful in the sense that they now know that they do not look as nervous as they thought they did. Knowing that their nervousness did not show helps them accept these naturally nervous feelings. *Never* apologize for feeling nervous. If you don't apologize, the audience may never know you were dying on the inside. During my workshops, we watch everyone's videos together as a group and we do group feedback along with professional feedback. When a participant watches his or her video, I often hear that person say, "I looked and felt so nervous." When another participant in the class says, "You didn't look nervous at all!" and everyone agrees, this is further validation to this speaker that his or her assumption that he or she looks nervous is not valid.

Now knowing that the nervousness is not as observable as originally thought—since this was validated by the class—the speaker's nervousness further reduces.

8. *Concentrate on your message and not the medium.* Your nervous feelings will quickly dissipate if you divert your attention away from your anxieties and instead concentrate on your message and having a conversation with your audience. Focus on Aspect 2: The Message.

9. *Turn nervousness into positive energy.* The same nervous energy that causes your speaking anxiety can be used as an asset to you as a presenter. Harness this energy and transform it into vitality and enthusiasm.

10. *Gain experience.* Experience builds confidence, which is the key to successful public speaking. Most speakers find that their anxiety will decrease more and more after each presentation they give. To avoid the "me-versus-them trap," think about your audience instead of yourself. Focus on having a conversation with your audience, and you will begin to see them as friendly and will become less nervous.

Remember four things in particular:

1. Identify your listeners. Know who they are before you speak.

2. Speak with passion about your subject; speak from the heart.

3. Communicate your excitement. Focus on wanting to tell your audience about your subject.

4. Remember who the expert is. *You* were the one who was asked to speak.

Following are some physical techniques you can use during your next presentation.

Physical Techniques to Help Reduce Speaking Anxiety

1. Don't fight nervousness directly. Accept it and ease your way through it.

2. Take a brisk walk before your presentation. This will help loosen up your entire body and get your blood circulating. It will also guarantee steadier knees.

3. Do not sit with your legs crossed, because one leg could cramp up or fall asleep.

4. While sitting, let your arms dangle comfortably at your sides.

5. While sitting, twist your wrists so your fingers shake loosely and gently.

6. Foster a feeling of security by pretending you're wearing an overcoat. Try to imagine you can feel its comforting weight on your shoulders.

7. To relax facial muscles, wriggle your jaw back and forth three of four times.

8. Do some deep breathing exercises for about two to five minutes. This will help release endorphins, which are among the brain chemicals known as neurotransmitters. They function to transmit electrical signals within the nervous system.

9. Say to yourself, "Let's go!"

Don't be self-conscious about having a warm-up routine. Athletes have a warm-up routine and speaking and giving a presentation is a physical activity. You can model your warm-up routing after this one provided or personalize your own to meet your needs and situation.

Mental Techniques to Help Reduce Speaking Anxiety

1. Prepare and rehearse. If you rehearse your presentation just once, you are doing more than 80 percent of presenters.
2. Think beyond the presentation to your goals and communicating your message.
3. Act your part.
4. Be enthusiastic.
5. Psyche yourself with positive, confident thoughts.
6. Use visualization to foster positive feelings.
7. Use isometric exercises to physically warm up.
8. Yawn.
9. Scrunch your toes. You need these to keep your proper balance.
10. Make purposeful movements during your presentation.
11. Project confidence and generosity and have fun.

ASPECT 7—THE SETTING

The setting is the place or location where you deliver your presentation and may be one that enhances or interferes with the effectiveness of your presentation. Whenever you can, you need to determine what the facilities are like *before* you deliver your presentation. Knowing as much about your presentation setting can make or break your success of your presentation. The more you know in advance of your presentation, the better you can properly plan your delivery and make any adjustments with your presentation.

Whenever possible, take the time to actually visit the location and the specific room where you will be speaking in advance. Find out from the meeting planner, meeting organizer, hotel staff, or person coordinating the meeting what the room layout will be. Not knowing this information can actually increase a presenter's speaking anxiety. Even little details such as getting the proper addresses and directions to where the meeting will be held are very important. When I am in a new city or location, I will even take a test drive from the hotel I am staying at to the location of the program, if it is not being held in the same hotel I am staying in. This allows me to get a better idea how long it will take to drive to this location. Keep in mind, if you do this on a Sunday and your program is that Monday, the actual drive time may be a lot longer due to Monday morning rush hour. You must take this into consideration.

Many professional speakers, including myself, provide a preferred meeting room layout for our presentations. When I am coordinating where I will be speaking, I always obtain as much detail about the physical setup of the room as possible. I typically fax over the preferred room arrangement, including seating in advance. Following are some additional items I usually discuss with the meeting planner or hotel staff:

1. Room location and room size and layout
2. Chair and table arrangements
3. Door locations
4. Stage or podium setup
5. Window locations
6. Lighting
7. Signage for my program
8. Hotel background music

9. Control of the room temperature

10. Other functions taking place during my program

11. Food arrangements

12. Arrangements for audiovisual equipment

13. Microphones

I will discuss each of these on the following pages.

Room Location and Room Size and Layout

How the room is arranged can make a huge difference in the success of your presentation. If your meeting is held in a company's conference room, you may not have much ability to adjust the seating arrangements. If you are delivering a presentation in a large auditorium with fixed seating, you also do not have much ability to make changes.

In most cases, though, you will be delivering your presentation in a hotel conference room or convention room. Here, you do have some options about how you want the room to be set up and arranged for your presentation. However, if you are one of several speakers, this may not be the case, as the association or meeting planner has already determined what the best set up will be for the meeting. When you do have the opportunity to set the room up for your presentation, you will have several options available to you.

On the following several pages, I have provided some illustrations for various room setups (see Figures 1.2 through 1.9). On the following few pages I have illustrated the four most common room arrangements I personally use. I have provided poor and better arrangements for each of the following types.

1. Classroom style

2. U-shaped style

3. Theater or lecture style

4. Dinner style

Classroom Style

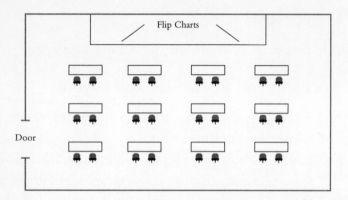

Figure 1.2   Poor Classroom Arrangement: The seating and tables do not allow the participants to make easy eye contact with you or each other.

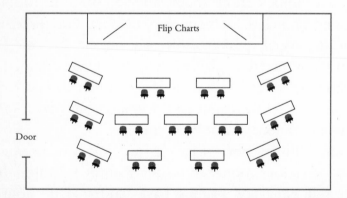

Figure 1.3   Better Classroom Arrangement: The seating and table are arranged in such a manner and allows the audience to see one another which will encourage better interaction between you and the audience.

U-Shaped Style

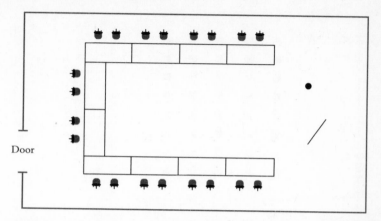

Figure 1.4   Poor U-Shaped Arrangement: This arrangement does not allow the presenter (indicated by the black dot) to be close enough to their audience.

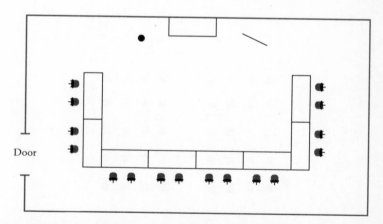

Figure 1.5   Better U-Shaped Arrangement: This arrangement allows the presenter (indicated by the black dot) to be closer to the audience and provides for a more relaxed atmosphere.

Theater or Lecture Style

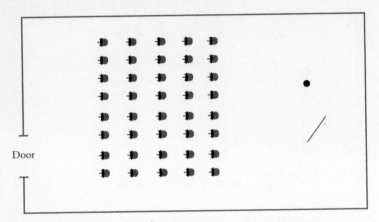

Figure 1.6 Poor Theater Arrangement:
This arrangement has the participants crammed together
and farther away from the presenter.

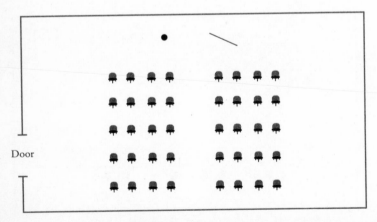

Figure 1.7 Better Theater Arrangement: This arrangement places the speaker closer to the audience and provides more space between the seating, including an aisle up the center to allow easier access.

Dinner Style

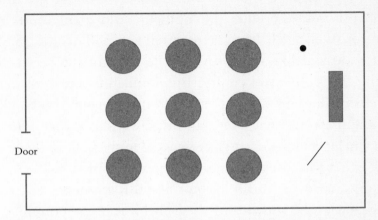

Figure 1.8   Poor Dinner Arrangement: Round tables are set up in perfect rows and will obstruct the audience's view of the presenter.

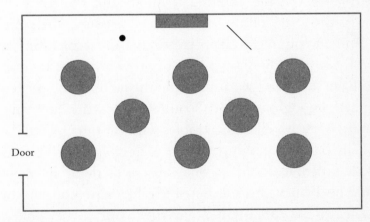

Figure 1.9   Better Dinner Arrangement: Round tables are staggered and prevent the participant's view from being blocked. This allows a better view of the speaker and the head table.

Table and Chair Arrangements

You should arrange the chairs in advance, creating the fewest number of rows as possible. Do not set up more tables and chairs than you will need. Most people tend to avoid sitting in the front rows and like to sit toward the back of the room, thus leaving the front rows empty. By eliminating any extra tables and chairs, this will ensure that the front rows will also be filled.

Some presenters will even put out fewer chairs than you will need and leave some extra chairs stacked in the back of the room. They believe this helps create the impression of a "full" seminar or workshop. I personally do not like this approach. If I was a participant in the audience, I don't feel it is my responsibility to set up chairs and the person arranging the room should know how many seats will be needed. If you find the room already set up when you arrive and you know there are too many chairs, you can tape the back few rows of chairs with "reserved" sign on them to force people entering to sit toward the front of the room. As the chairs fill up, have someone remove the signs and tape. Bringing out more chairs creates too much of a distraction.

If you are providing a workshop, provide tables; be mindful not to have too many seats at each of the tables. Each participant will need enough room to comfortably write and lay out materials. Most hotel seminar tables will seat three people, but I personally have only two people at each table. Forcing three or even four people to sit at one table will result in someone banging his or her knees against the table legs. You want your audience to be comfortable. Provide your participants with comfortable chairs, especially if they will be with you for a few days. They will appreciate it. Allow plenty of room between the tables and chairs to allow people to easily get up and move around. There is nothing worse than being crammed into a small room. This is especially true if you are also providing refreshments during your program. The important thing is to make it as comfortable for your audience as you can.

Door Locations

When you can, try to arrange the room in such a manner that the tables and chairs face away from the entrance and exit doors. This will allow people to quietly slip in and out without interrupting you.

Should you decide to provide refreshments during your program, I recommend that you set these up in the back of the room, where most breaks will take place. People can easily grab their refreshments as they come and go from the room. If you provide seminars, you can also sell some of your products if you have a table set up in the back of the room for this purpose. This will allow people to look at your materials while on breaks. I even go so far as to tape the door latches on the door to eliminate the noise made by opening and closing the door. I am sure many of you have attended a conference and the door you just opened or closed made a loud noise as the door latch clicked.

Window Locations

Whenever you can, try to have the room arranged such that any windows are at the back of the room. This needs to be coordinated well in advance. I have been in a situation where I was speaking to a large group of salespeople and directly in back of me was a large set of picture windows overlooking the gorgeous golf course behind me. If curtains are available, have them drawn closed to remove this external distraction. If you are early in the planning phases of organizing a room for your presentation, visit the room and check out the layout. If you do not like the room layout, ask if another room is available or if you can swap rooms with someone else.

Lighting

Proper lighting is very important to the success of your presentation. People need to be able to easily see you. Check out the room's lighting the evening before your meeting or presentation. Locate where all the lighting controls are for the room. Spend some time learning what switch turns the lights on and which switch turns them off. Some hotel rooms even have special switches that easily creates a select lighting combination. Check them all out and determine which one will work best for your setup. I sometimes even label the light switches so that any last-minute changes can easily be made.

Never let yourself, as the presenter, be in complete darkness. Check out the wall sconces and make sure there are none directly behind you. A few years back, I was attending a large convention and I was sitting in the same room I was scheduled to speak in the next day. While I sat there, listening to the presenter, I noticed some strategically located lights on the wall behind the presenter. These wall lights were very bright and were a distraction to me. I made a mental note of this and prior to my presentation the next day, I arrived early and loosened the bulbs in these wall sconces so they were not lit when I spoke.

As the speaker, you are the one responsible for the setting. The preceding are just a few examples of what I do to control and minimize any external distractions during my presentation.

Hotel Background Music

Many hotel or conference centers routinely have light background music playing. This music is often also playing in the conference rooms. You should check to see if you can turn this music off yourself or if you need someone to do this for you. In most cases, it involves a simple switch that needs to be turned off; however, this switch may be in another room.

Several times a year, I travel to the Middle East, mostly to Dubai, UAE, where I provide four to five days of training. I always arrive a day or so earlier to allow my internal clock to adjust to the new time zone and to also check on the room setup for my program. Some of the conference rooms I have used in a few of the Dubai hotels have their lighting and sound controls for the room in a master closet in the hall. Some of the controls in one room I was speaking in were in the same room but the remainder were located in the conference room office. I needed to learn where all the controls were in order to completely control the room lighting and sound.

Room Temperature Controls

It is important that the room you are presenting in be comfortable for your audience. Find out from the hotel or convention hall how to control the room temperature. Many hotel rooms and convention centers have thermostats that are locked behind a Plexiglas cover. Ask if the cover can be unlocked and removed during your program. If the hotel is unwilling to do this, as some are, get the name and phone number of hotel personnel or manager who can make adjustments. Sometimes when I arrive early to a room, the temperature of the room is just perfect. I show up early the next day and the room is now either freezing or is like a sauna. The key is to arrive early enough so that you, as the presenter, can make the adjustments in the room temperature.

Other Function at the Same Location

Delivering a presentation is difficult enough. Take the time to find out if there are any other functions going on during your program in the next room. Sometimes you are in one large room divided only by a folding partition; in such cases, the sound from each side of that partition will be heard by the people sitting on the other side. If you find out that there may be a large function, such as a wedding or some other noisy conference, see if you can move the location of your program. I have been able to do this several times over my career. Many times, the hotel will be able to work with you.

Meeting or Presentation Delivered On-Site at a Company

I provide several of my workshops and seminars on-site at a client's corporate location. You may need to arrive early to allow time to sign in at security, have someone escort you to the room, and help you set up for your meeting or presentation. You will want to verify, well ahead of time, where you will be meeting someone, whether you get into the building earlier to set up, and who will agree to meet you there early and help you set up. I do a lot of training and workshops for the Army, and they have several additional security and access requirements just to get on base. What additional requirements will you need to be able to get on-site at your client's facility? All of this has to deal with the setting, and it is your responsibility, as the presenter, to know what is required of you. If you do not know this well in advance, you may be delayed at security and late for your presentation, or worse, you may not be allowed on site. That can be very embarrassing.

Food and Refreshment Arrangements and Breaks

If you are planning to have food served as part of your function, make sure your attendees know this in advance. You may want to allow some time in your schedule for people to mingle and greet one another before your program starts. You need to build this time into your day's schedule. You also want to factor in what you will be providing during your breaks.

It is a good idea to have some coffee, tea, juice, pastry, and fresh fruit in the morning. Many people "need" their coffee fix first thing in the morning and will have a headache by mid-morning if you do not make it available. Soda, water, and juices are a good idea to have in the afternoon, along with some light snack.

If you are not providing lunch as part of your meeting, ask the hotel if they will be; if not, you may need to arrange for someone to bring food in. You can also coordinate with the hotel to have a section within the hotel's restaurant reserved for your group. If you are having food brought in, you need to coordinate the time and what will be required to get the food brought to you and set up. Did you have a table in the room for this purpose? If you decide people are on their own and will need to go out for lunch, be sure to allow enough time for them to travel, eat, and return. I will usually arrange to have the hotel provide a list of local restaurants and their menus so that people can review their options just prior to lunch.

Audio Visual Requirements

It is always a good idea to make sure that all your audiovisual requirements have been arranged. Do not assume that just because you asked or even sent the hotel or client your setup requirements that everything will be there set up as you requested. As many years as I have been speaking professionally, this is one area that never seems to change. What you ask for, regardless of how far in advance you ask for it, may not always be there. This is why it is so critical for you to arrive early and verify you have everything you need.

I often bring my own equipment, including some backup supplies. This way, I know I have all the equipment I need, I know it works, and I do not have to find someone to get me that LCD projector I asked for two months ago. Get to your speaking venue early so that you can set up and make any last-minute changes if something is not right. If the hotel forgets something, it is now your problem to resolve.

■ ■ ■

At the start of this chapter, I said that in order to be a successful speaker, you need to learn and understand all seven of the aspects I just talked about. You need to deal with all these aspects at the same time. The seven aspects again are:

Aspect 1—The Speaker

Aspect 2—The Message

Aspect 3—The Audience

Aspect 4—The Channel

Aspect 5—The Feedback

Aspect 6—The Noise

Aspect 7—The Setting

CHAPTER 2

Gathering Information and Materials

The most difficult and also the most important part of making a presentation is determining how to actually start. Many presenters worry themselves sick trying to figure out how to get started and what exactly they want to say. My advice is to not worry about how you are going to start. Your first step in preparing your presentation is to collect and read as much information as possible about your subject. Learn as much about your topic as you can. Prepare detailed notes on some of the ideas you may want to use during your presentation. Ask yourself what information you plan on discussing during your presentation, what message you want to deliver to your audience, and where you can find additional information.

You should first select a topic that interests you and one you have some knowledge about or have an interest in becoming knowledgeable about. You should also pick a topic that will interest your audience. The first place I always like to draw from is my own personal experience. Most people have more expertise and experiences than they realize. I recommend that you sit down and brainstorm or mind map out what you already know.

One great source, which is grossly underused, is your local library. The use of the Internet (which I will talk about later) has made it easy for people to avoid going to their local library. If you do not have a library card or you have not been to your local library for some time, I suggest you get back into a routine of visiting your local library. If it has been awhile since you last used your local library, you may need someone to show you the modern tools you now have available for doing your research and gathering information.

Some of the best resources available at your local library are:

- Librarians
- Catalogs
- Periodicals
- Newspapers
- Reference works

Let's take a brief look at each one of these.

LIBRARIANS

Your local librarian is a wonderful source to start with. They have an enormous amount of experience, can identify the resources available to you, and can point you in the right direction to start your research. Some resources can be checked out and taken home for a short period of time; other resources can only be viewed and used at the library. Bring a pad and pen with you to take notes. Most libraries have copy machines and allow you to make some copies of certain types of documents. This can save you a lot of writing time.

CATALOGS

A key tool you need to familiarize yourself with is the library catalog. The old days, when I was many years younger than I am today, we had what was called the card catalog. This was literally a filing cabinet with small card catalog drawers that were arranged in alphabetical order. You would search for your topic using the cards. On each printed card would be a resource (a book, magazine, periodical) and the location of this resource within the library. You would write down as many of the resources along with their location within the library. Today's modern library has replaced this card system with a computer that can search several databases for the information you are looking for. It will also usually tell you if this resource is available or already signed out by someone. This computerized system is very similar to those used in your large bookstores today. The process is the same.

The library electronic catalog will also allow you to search other libraries if your local library does not have the information you are looking for.

PERIODICALS

Another wonderful resource available to you is the periodical database. This database contains hundreds of thousands of articles and publications from a large variety of journals, magazines, and publications. Much of the recent and past research done within universities is published in a number of journals, each specific to a particular type of industry. When you are looking to find some good published material to reference for your presentation, this is great place to look.

NEWSPAPERS

Your local library will also have a section with several of the various local and national newspapers. They usually have the current paper along with some of the recent and past newspaper publications. On the morning of all my presentations, I look at some of the local newspapers in my area (or the area I may be speaking at). You will be amazed how many times you will find a timely article related to your presentation. When I find such an article, I will bring that publication with me to my presentation (if I can) and I will read from it. This not only serves as a good visual aid and prop, it also visually adds credibility to the information you read from the publication. When your audience sees you read from a source, they more readily accept that information. If that newspaper happens to be that morning's newspaper, then you automatically have shown you have used the most current data.

REFERENCE WORKS

Several types of reference works are available. All of these sources have information collected and organized in an easy-to-use and easy-access format. Two of the most popular types of reference work are:

- *Encyclopedias:* I was ever so fortunate to have these at home. (I remember when I was a kid, my parents spent a ton of money on encyclopedias, including the annual updated volume.) It was like having my own private library. A man would go door-to-door selling encyclopedias. He loved our house because my parents seem to buy all of them. Lucky for me.

- *Books of quotations:* A number of books devoted just to quotations are available. Some even contain nothing but humorous quotations. Finding just the right quotation for your presentation can add that special flare you are looking for.

THE INTERNET

The amount of information available to you today on the Internet is staggering. You can find the exact information you are looking for with a few clicks of your mouse. The Internet has changed how people do research and has had a big impact on your local library. You are actually able to search your local library's database online without leaving your house. In fact, you can search libraries from all over the world and then request to have the book or resource sent to your local library, where you can pick it up. There are many Internet tools you can use, such as search engines, online databases, virtual libraries, and even private publications. Like any other resource, you need to verify and validate the information you find; there is a lot of incorrect information online as well.

Regardless of which resources you use, the process from here remains the same. You have to select the information to use and then decide how much of it you will include in your presentation. To accomplish this, you need to know how long your presentation will be. The amount you will be able to discuss in a one-hour presentation differs from the amount you will talk about in a full-day workshop or even a 15-minute overview presentation. The level of the detail may be different in each case; however, the format or structure of your presentation should be the same in all cases.

Deciding on the format is your next challenge. It is at this point that you need to decide how much material you will use and in what sequence you will present the material you have chosen. How much material you comfortably present will depend on the length of your presentation. At this point, I am talking only about the main content of your presentation, not the entire presentation. We have not talked about introductions or closings. For now, I am talking only about the body of your presentation.

How much time you actually need to present your information will depend on the allotted time limit for your presentation. I will discuss allotted times in Chapter 3, but for the purpose of this discussion, let's assume the body of our presentation (your main points) will use 50 percent of the total allotted time. Following are suggested time limits, based on how much time you are limited to. I have provided these suggestions only as a general guidance for your presentation.

Number of Main Points	Suggested Time Limit Needed for Body
4 points	10 minutes
5—6 points	15 minutes
7—8 points	30 minutes

Remember, the times provided here are for the body of your presentation. If you then take the time allocated for the body (e.g., 15 minutes) and double it, this would give you a total presentation time of 30 minutes. A presentation that will cover seven to eight points would require a total time of 60 minutes, 30 minutes of which would be to cover those seven to eight points. This will allow sufficient time for you to develop a proper introduction and allow for questions at the end as part of your conclusion. Chapter 3 will discuss time limits and how they fit into the complete structure of the presentation in more detail.

When you are gathering information for your presentation, you need to gather more information than you need to cover during your allotted time limit. That's okay. The additional information you gather may come in handy during the presentation or during the question–and–answer period.

There are several other considerations you need to take into account as you gather your materials and do your research for your presentation. Some of these considerations are not even addressed by many presenters during their presentation preparation phase. Let's look at some of these.

WHAT VISUAL AIDS WILL YOU USE DURING YOUR PRESENTATION? WILL YOU USE ANY VISUAL AIDS?

The visual aids you decide to make and use during your presentation will either support your verbal message or not. I will discuss the use of visual aids in more detail in Chapter 4.

WHERE WILL YOU STAND DURING YOUR PRESENTATION?

You need to decide where you will actually stand when you deliver your presentation. Will you be standing on a stage, talking from behind a lectern, or seated around the long table in a large executive boardroom? As the presenter, you decide where you want to stand. Just because someone has set up a lectern in the room does not mean that you have to speak from this lectern; however, this may be the only location where they have a microphone.

If you need a microphone but do not want to stand behind the lectern, it is your responsibility to find this out ahead of time and let the meeting planner or organizer know you need a wireless or handheld microphone. These are details you need to determine before your presentation. Many presenters don't even inquire about these details.

When asked to give a presentation, the first thing some people think about is, "What am I going to wear?" "Will there be a lot of people there?" "What if I mess up?" Although these are important questions, they represent only one small part of your presentation. Several components need to be taken into consideration when preparing a presentation. Some may ask themselves, "What if my presentation is not good enough?" If we construct our presentations with care and properly prepare and practice, our presentations will always be good. Do not be afraid to take risks and present new material. Remember, *practice makes perfect.*

PRESENTATION PREPARATION AS A PROCESS

Genuine presentation preparation means you need to dig something out of yourself. You need to gather all the facts and arrange your thoughts. It is not enough to simply collect ideas. You must also nurture these ideas and reflect on how to present them in a unique, organized manner.

Your presentation needs time to develop and grow. You should prepare for weeks, sleep on your topic, and let the ideas mull around in your mind. Dream about your ideas and let your ideas sink into your subconscious. Ask yourself questions. Write down your thoughts. Keep a pad and paper near your nightstand so that you can write your brilliant ideas when you think about them in the middle of the night. If you do not write them down, there is no guarantee you will remember them in the morning when you wake up. Take a pad of paper and a pen with you when you are out walking the dog, going for a walk, and going out to dinner. These are the times when those ideas seem to pop into my head.

Once you have determined the purpose for your presentation and the main message, state that purpose and message in a sentence and begin building your presentation around that message. Ask yourself, "How does this purpose relate to my audience?" Let your purpose drive your presentation.

Some other questions you may want to consider asking yourself are:

1. In one concise sentence, what is the purpose of this presentation?

2. Who will be in the audience? What is their main interest in this topic?

3. What do I really know and believe about this topic as it relates to this audience? What additional research can I do?

4. What are the main points of my outline?

5. What relevant information and stories can I use to support each of my main points?

6. What visual aids, if any, do I need?

7. Do I have an effective opening grabber?

8. In my closing, how do I intend to answer my listeners' question, "What's in it for me?"

9. Have I polished and prepared the language and words I will use?

10. Have I prepared a written a concise introduction for myself?

11. Have I taken care of the small details that will help me speak more confidently?

INFORMATION OVERLOAD

Frequently, a presenter will attempt to provide too much information during a presentation. Avoid using too many facts, figures, and lists. Most technical presentations are flawed in this manner. They are usually too complex and packed with data.

The presenter who is delivering the presentation is so enthusiastic about their topic he or she feels the need to share everything he or she knows in this one presentation. Having been an engineer for more than 25 years, I can testify firsthand that this was the case in many engineering conferences. Many presenters would try to present 60 minutes' worth of material in a 30-minute window. One of the biggest challenges with preparing any presentation is to determine how much material you are able to use. This becomes easier with experience, and when we discuss structure of a presentation in Chapter 3, this will become clearer to you.

When I am preparing for a new presentation, workshop, or keynote, I use folders to collect my ideas and thoughts as I do my research. I also find it helpful to write down where I got my material so I am able to go back to the source if needed. If you find an article, written by someone else, that you find helpful and would like to use some of that material, you need to make certain you obtain permission from the author. I receive requests all the time to use my published articles and some of their content. A simple e-mail or phone call will usually suffice, but I recommend you have the person sign a permission or release form for your records. This protects you and the other party.

One area you also need to be very careful with is using graphics or cartoons you find on the Internet. I see many presenters include a favorite cartoon within their presentation. Presenters often do not realize that they need written permission to do so. In some cases, you may be required to pay a small licensing fee to use that cartoon or photograph. Using other people's material without permission is a copyright infringement and can get you into serious trouble. The Internet has made it very easy for people to steal and plagiarize articles.

I was speaking as the closing keynote speaker for a conference a few years ago and had the opportunity to listen to a speaker earlier in the morning. He was using statistics and information from many sources and trying to pass on this information off as his own. I had the chance to speak with him after his presentation and asked him where he got his information and data.

I also told him that some of the information he used was information published by someone else and asked him if he had permission to use the data. He said to me that his theory was, if he used one person's information, that was plagiarism, and if he used everyone's information, that was research. I could not believe what I just heard.

Should you decide to use information and work developed by other people, get their permission and give them proper credit for that information. A simple mention of the person's name by way of a footnote would suffice. A better way is to get written permission, which will allow you to say, "Used by permission," but still also state the source of the information.

USING VIDEOS AND MUSIC DURING YOUR PRESENTATION

Many presentations today also include the use of videos within their presentations. This is becoming increasingly common. A presenter finds a video that has a scene that perfectly illustrates a point he or she is trying to make and adds it to the presentation. You see the use of videos a lot during training sessions and workshops. I am sure you have all experienced this. A presenter shows a short clip from a video they purchased for home use. They think they can bring this video in and use it during their presentation. This is actually a performance copyright violation. The video was purchased for "home use." It was not purchased for public viewing. A presenter needs to get permission to use this video in a public forum. The presenter thinks that because he or she purchased the video and now owns it that he or she has permission to use this video during a presentation. Take a look at the personal videos at home, and you will notice that it states on the packaging and the video itself for "Personal use only."

You need to get permission from the author of this video if you want to use it in your presentation.

The same problem occurs when presenters decide to use music during their workshops or presentations. You also need to get permission to use this copyrighted music. Some speakers who have violated both these copyright infringements have found themselves on the wrong end of the law and were heavily fined or even arrested. You must obtain permission.

CHAPTER 3

The Structure of a Presentation

All presentations should be organized into three major sections, regardless of length:

1. The introduction
2. The body
3. The conclusion

Let's take a look at each section in greater detail.

THE INTRODUCTION

The introduction is the beginning of your presentation and should account for 10 to 15 percent of your total presentation time. For purposes of this section, let's assume you are scheduled to give a 60-minute presentation. Fifteen percent of 60 minutes is 9 minutes. This means the introduction section of your presentation should take only about 9 minutes.

Your introduction consists of three parts:

1. The grabber
2. The purpose
3. The agenda

The *grabber* is an opening statement to grab the attention of the audience. This may include such things as a quote, a shocking statistic, or some startling statement. You may also use a humorous quote. I do not, however, recommend using a joke. Most jokes take too long to tell. Most presenters are lousy joke tellers, and most jokes have nothing to do with your presentation. Many presenters think (and even believe) they need to start off with a joke to "loosen up" the audience, when in fact it is them, the presenters, who need to loosen up. Your average short joke takes several minutes to tell, and in most cases, it does not get the expected reaction from the audience.

There is nothing wrong with including humor in your presentation, but using a joke will generally take too long. You are better off using a humorous quote, but find a quote that pertains to your presentation. There are books and many resources you can use for humorous quotes.

Here is an example of a humorous quote I have used during some of my workshops. One section of my presentation skills workshop has to deal with speaking anxiety, and I usually begin this section with the following quote:

> Mark Twain said it best, "There are two types of speakers. Those that are nervous and those that are liars." Which one are you?

This usually results in a chuckle or two from the participants in my workshop.

You can also use a shocking statistic or ask a rhetorical question as part of your grabber. Think about what you use now. The introduction is the one area many presenters do not put much thought into and really should. A good introduction gives your audience an idea of what you will be presenting and why it is important to listen to you. Your audience wants to know, "What's in it for me? Why should I listen?"

The second part of your introduction is the *purpose*. Ask yourself, "What is the purpose of my presentation?" You can state, "The purpose of my presentation is to . . ." The purpose is tied to your message. You do not need to have a visual aid that shows this statement; just say it.

The last part of the introduction is the *agenda*. You should always provide you audience with an agenda of your presentation.

Your audience wants and needs to know what you are going to talk about. Most presentations fail to include an agenda, but by not having one, it becomes easy to get off track and not follow a logical flow of information. A well-thought-out agenda provides you with a plan or sequence for your presentation.

THE BODY

The middle section of your presentation is the main body of your presentation. This is the part of your presentation where you present or discuss your main ideas and key points. The body should account for 70 to 80 percent of your total presentation time. For a 60-minute presentation, 70 to 80 percent is about 45 minutes. This is where you provide your key points and ideas, in other words, the meat of your presentation. The number of points you discuss again depends on the length of your presentation. I talked about this in Chapter 2 when I discussed gathering information. Referring back to that section, you will see that I recommend limiting the number of key points to seven to eight for a 60-minute presentation. In a 45-minute time frame, you would have approximately 6 minutes for each key point. Keep in mind, some points may need more or less time for your discussion, but the total time frame allocated for the body of your talk is 45 minutes. As you prepare the content of each of these points, keep in mind the level of detail you will need to stay within the time allocation of this section.

An Alternative Approach

One alternative approach for discussion during the body of your presentation is to use an acronym to get your key points across. An acronym is a set or combination of letters used to define a phrase. There are times when I like to use an actual word as an acronym for developing the content for the body of my presentation. Here is an example.

Several years ago I was hired to deliver the closing keynote for a large international sales team during their National Sales meeting, which was held at a major ski resort in Vermont. I was hired on very short notice and was to deliver this 60-minute closing keynote the following week. Normally, companies hire professional speakers well in advance, but the originally scheduled speaker for this event had some family emergency at the last minute and had to cancel only a few days before the event. Being familiar with me and knowing I would be able to step in at the last minute, the original speaker suggested the client contact me. The client called me on a Friday, and I was to be up at Mount Snow, Vermont, the following Tuesday to deliver this closing keynote. You do the math . . . this was not a lot of time.

It turned out I was available and was glad to step in and help this client. We talked over the phone, and they said they wanted me to motivate and inspire their sales team to go out and be more successful. They asked if I had a keynote that matched this objective. I told them I would deliver a customized presentation that would convey this message. They asked me what the title of the presentation was, and not having actually developed it yet, I said, without hesitation, "The Motivation to I.N.S.P.I.R.E." They said this sounded perfect. I then spent the next two days developing and customizing a 60-minute keynote around the acronym I.N.S. P.I.R.E. Because this keynote was being delivered at a ski resort in Vermont, I also decide to weave in the theme of skiing and tie into my presentation the challenges of skiing and how we can use an analogy of those challenges to be successful. I arrived the evening before my keynote and had the opportunity to network with some of the attendees and gather some additional insights about the group I would be speaking to the next day.

Without telling you about the entire keynote, here is how I used the acronym I.N.S.P.I.R.E. to develop my keynote for this client. I assigned a key idea or thought for each letter of the word and spoke extemporaneously around each idea:

"I" stands for importance

"N" stands for needs

"S" stands for success

"P" stands for passion

"I" stands for influence

"R" stands for results

"E" stands for enthusiasm

As I presented each key point, I tied the presentation into the word *inspire*, thereby creating an anchor to tie my message to. When they think about the word *inspire*, they will now think about my message and remember my presentation. You can use this same approach and use an acronym, or even a word or slogan, and develop your presentation around each letter of the acronym. It does require a little more creativity, but it is well worth it in the end.

THE CONCLUSION

The last section of your presentation is the conclusion and should account for 10 to 15 percent of your total presentation time. The conclusion is divided into three parts:

1. The review
2. The call to action
3. The closing grabber

During the *review* you want to reiterate the purpose of your presentation and highlight the answers to the audience's question, "What's in it for me?" The review provides you with one more opportunity to drive home your main message. As part of your review, you can go back and review the agenda you provided at the beginning and provide a brief highlight for each key point you discussed during your presentation. Remember, this is a high-level review, not a repeat of your detailed presentation.

The second part of your conclusion is the *call to action* segment. This segment is where you tell your audience what you want them to do with the information you just presented. This is where you can provide a specific list of action items or specific things you want your audience to do as a result of your presentation. This is their *call to action*.

The last part of your conclusion is the *closing grabber*. The *closing grabber* could be a short statement or quote that ties the entire presentation back to your message. This includes any closing remarks and should leave your audience with at least one memorable thought. This is your last chance to drive your message home and leave a lasting impression. In some cases, I have even combined my closing thought with a more theatrical closing, one that involves props or even a costume or dramatic visual aid. By doing this, I plant an anchor in the audience's mind to help them remember my message.

MONROE'S MOTIVATED SEQUENCE— SPECIAL FORMAT FOR SALES PRESENTATIONS

One other special format that can be used for a persuasive presentation is Monroe's motivated sequence. Monroe's motivated sequence is a special technique used to organize a persuasive presentation that inspires people to take action. This special sequence was developed by Alan H. Monroe in the mid-1930s. Alan Monroe was a professor at Purdue University. Professor Monroe developed this time-proven method for organizing persuasive presentations.

The method consists of five steps:

1. Step 1: Get attention (attention step).
2. Step 2: Establish a need (need step).
3. Step 3: Satisfy that need (satisfaction step).
4. Step 4: Visualize the future (visualization step).
5. Step 5: Take action/actualization (action step).

A simplified format may be:

1. *Attention:* Hey, listen to me. I have a problem!
2. *Need:* Let me explain the problem.
3. *Satisfaction:* I have the solution to my problem.
4. *Visualization:* If I implement my solution, this is what will happen.
5. *Action:* Here is how you can help me. Are you willing to help?

Let's take a more detailed look at each of these steps.

Step 1: Get attention (attention step): Get the attention of your audience by using a grabber such as a story, humor, or a shocking statistic that will encourage the audience to pay attention. This step is part of the presentation's introduction section. You still need to describe the purpose of your presentation and let your audience know what to expect.

Step 2: Establish a need (need step): During this step is when you convince your audience there is a problem or situation that needs a change. This is where you should use some statistics to back up your statements. Talk about what will happen or can happen if a change is not made and show a need for action to be taken.

Step 3: Satisfy that need (satisfaction step): This is when you discuss how this need can be satisfied and offer your solution to the problem. This is the main section of your presentation and will vary greatly depending on the specific purpose of your presentation. Discuss the facts and elaborate enough so that your audience understands your solution. Use examples, testimonials, and statistics to support your solution.

Step 4: Visualize the future (visualization step): Describe to the audience what will happen when and if they implement or do not implement your solution. The more realistic and detailed you can make the vision, the stronger the desire will be to implement your solution. Help them visualize what the situation would be like after they have implemented your solution.

There are three approaches you can take to do this:

a. Positive method: Outline what the situation would be like if your ideas are adopted.

b. Negative method: Describe what the situation would be like if your ideas are not adopted.

c. Contrast method: Describe the negative picture first, and then describe what could happen if they accept your ideas.

Step 5: Take action/actualization (action step): The final step is to leave your audience specific action steps they can take to solve the problem. You want to convince them to take action immediately.

Monroe's motivated sequence is the best approach used by successful sales professionals and follows the process of human thinking and leads the audience step by step to the desired action. This is the most effective technique used by advertisers, TV commercials, and people who make their living persuading others.

The advantage of Monroe's motivated sequence is that it emphasizes what the audience can do. It shows the audience that they actually have the ability to take some actions and make a change.

THE DOZEN DEADLY DANGERS— REASONS FOR POOR PRESENTATIONS

Following are my top 12 reasons presentations do not succeed. I call them the dozen deadly dangers.

1. *No real clear objectives:* This goes back to my earlier discussion about knowing your message before you start to develop your presentation. Most presentations fail because the message is not clear to presenter. If the message is not clear to the presenter, it certainly will not be clear to the audience.

2. *Poor preparation:* Too many presenters today do not know how to properly prepare for their presentations. In most cases, they were not taught. When I talk about presentation I like to refer to my nine Ps:

Prior **P**roper **P**reparation **P**revents **P**oor **P**erformance of the **P**erson **P**utting on the **P**resentation

Nothing will relax you more than to know you are properly prepared.

3. *No script:* Too many presenters do not have a plan or script of what they want to say. Many of us have sat through a bad movie and said to ourselves, this movie had no script. This same problem happens with presentations all the time.

4. *Fuzzy opening:* How you open or start your presentation is very important. You need to give you audience a clear idea of where you will be taking them. Let them know what to expect.

5. *Loss of focus during the body of the presentation:* When you do not have a clear message for your presentation and a clear objective, it is easy to get sidetracked. Not only does your message need to be clear, but it also needs to be threaded through your entire presentation.

6. *Lack of concern about the audience:* All effective presenters keep their audiences in mind during the development and delivery of their presentations. The wrong presentation delivered to the right audience is just as ineffective as the right presentation delivered to the wrong audience.

   It has been said, "Nobody cares how much you know, until they know how much you care."

7. *Poor visual aids:* Your visual aids should be designed to *aid* your presentation. Many times, presenters confuse their audiences when their visual aids are not easily understood. Visual aids can be either too busy or too complicated, leaving the audience unable to follow the presentation. At

the same time, you do not need to use a visual aid for every key point you are trying to make.

8. *Weak evidence:* Many times, presenters fail to provide substantial evidence for claims or statistics they use in their presentations. You should always state the source of your information. If you are quoting statistics from someone, credit that person for the information. Also do not use information you do not understand and have not verified through other independent sources. If you are not sure or question the data, do not use it.

9. *Poor delivery:* For presentations to be accepted by the audience, the audience first needs to accept the presenter. A presenter who is liked and trusted is more likely to have his or her ideas and information accepted. How you deliver your presentation is just as important as what you deliver. You have heard the expression, "It's not what you said, but how you said it." Your delivery is critical if you want your audience to accept your ideas and information.

10. *Negative attitude:* there is nothing worse than a poor attitude. Presenters with poor attitudes are not liked. Your attitude really shows when you present. Here is a great anonymous quote I have used for years to summarize this point:

> Your attitude more than your aptitude will determine your altitude.

11. *Anticlimactic ending:* As a presenter, your role is to lead your audience on a journey during your presentation. During your presentation, you build an expectation for the audience, and when you do not meet this expectation,

you leave them disappointed. It is like watching a dramatic movie that has an unexpected, or worse, disappointing, ending. It can upset the audience.

12. *No follow-up:* There is nothing worse than making a promise to get back to someone about a question and not doing so. When you agree to get in touch with someone, you need to make sure you follow up with that person as promised.

CHAPTER 4

Use of Visual Aids

When you prepare a presentation, you need to keep in mind how much information the audience can actually absorb through their senses. The amount of information an audience can retain will depend on the verbal aspect, the tone used, and the nonverbal aspect of your presentation.

In the 1960s, UCLA professor Dr. Albert Mehrabian conducted a series of experiments with college students. He wanted to test the power of body language, such as facial expressions, and how it compares to the words used in communicating the speaker's attitude and feelings when there is an inconsistency between the verbal and nonverbal clues.

In the first series of experiments, only one recorded word was spoken to the students to communicate whether the speaker liked, disliked, or was neutral toward the listener. The experimental subjects listened to a total of nine such words. Three words, *honey, dear*, and *thanks*, were used to indicate the speaker liked the listener. Three other words, *brute, don't*, and *terrible*, were used to denote that the speaker disliked the listener. Finally the words *maybe, really*, and *oh* were supposed to represent a neutral attitude. The speakers were instructed to vary their tone of voice three times while speaking each of these words. One time, the speaker's tone of voice was to reflect disliking, another time liking, and still another time neutrality. The statistical results showed that tone of voice was far more important in influencing the subjects' judgments of the true feelings of the speaker than the words themselves.

In another series of experiments, the researchers added another feature. The subjects were shown photographs with different facial expressions. The subjects were asked to guess the speaker's feelings based on these facial expressions. This time the facial expressions were found to be the greatest influence in the subjects' guessing the feelings behind the speaker's communications of the words. In combining the statistical results of these studies, the researchers came up with the 55 percent, 38 percent, and 7 percent rule, meaning that in 55 percent of the cases, the listener's judgment of the speaker's real feelings is based on facial expression (or other body language); in 38 percent of cases, it is based on tone of voice; and in only 7 percent of the cases, it is based on the words themselves.

Mehrabian and his colleagues published the results in May and June 1967 in two journals: *Journal of Personality and Social Psychology* and the *Journal of Consulting Psychology*. Mehrabian also mentions these studies in two books he published: *Silent Messages* (1971) and *Nonverbal Communication* (1972).

Although some researchers believe the statistics have been misquoted and misused, other studies outlined in Mehrabian's book *Silent Messages* suggested additional work that supported these results.

VALIDITY OF THE DATA

Although the validity of the actual numbers is questioned by some, what is agreed is that nonverbal communication and the tone of your voice has a much larger impact of the audience. What is also true is that all three clues in communicating with others are essential. Words, tone of voice, and body language not only must be consistent with one another but must actually support one another. If not, one may easily cancel out the other.

Although the application of these numbers to presentations has been discussed and debated by many people, most of the debate is focused around applying these numbers to all speaking situations. In all cases, people do agree that your nonverbal communication has a significantly higher influence on the listener than your words. If your nonverbal and verbal messages do not agree, you are sending a conflicting message. And when this is the case, most audiences will lean toward accepting the nonverbal message over the verbal message.

Think about it: how many times have you had a conversation with your significant other and you question what he or she is saying based on the conflict between what is being said and the expression on that person's face?

Although the 7 percent, 38 percent, and 55 percent numbers have been quoted and misused by many people, the bottom line is to keep in mind that your nonverbal messages can have a bigger impact on your audience than your words. As a presenter, be careful in quoting numbers and statistics, unless you know that background of the data. What is twisted or slanted truth yesterday, very quickly can become the truth today. If as a presenter you do not know where the data come from, then do not use them as fact.

USE OF VISUAL AIDS

Why do we use visual aids during presentations? Visual aids are used to improve or enhance our verbal message. A presentation involving the use of visual aids typically is more effective than a presentation that does not. This does assume, for the moment, that the visual aid being used enhances the message and does not confuse the listener. Your visual aid and your verbal message must be in agreement with each other.

Let's take a look at five important benefits of using visual aids and how they can help your presentations be more effective.

Benefit 1: Visual aids help clarify the information. Many of us have heard the expression "A picture says a thousand words," and we all know that it is easier to understand something when a visual aid is used in conjunction with any verbal description. If a presenter said, "I have this round ball," while at the same time holding a round ball, we automatically get a better idea of the actual round ball the presenter is talking about. Its size, color, and type, although not included in the verbal description, provide us, the audience, more information about the round ball.

Benefit 2: Visual aids save you time. As a presenter, using visual aids not only helps the audience better understand your message but also saves you time. Using visual aids show the audience that you are prepared and have taken the time to prepare some visual aids to use during your presentation and keep you on track. Try to deliver the same presentation without the use of your visual aids, and you may find yourself occasionally going off on some tangent during your presentation. This happens all the time with many presenters. Perhaps you have even been in an audience when a speaker does go off on a tangent and stops using or following the information on the visual aid— speakers can easily be taken off path during their pre- sentations when this happens. Using visual aids shows your audience you are organized and have a script (a visual script) you will be following.

Benefit 3: Visual aids help promote attentiveness. Using visual aids helps keep your audience awake. It does not matter how good a presenter you may be, you will eventually bore you audience if all you do is verbally talk to them and do not use any kind of visual aid. Don't get me wrong; there are many speakers who can be very engaging, pulling the audience to the edges of their seats through speaking alone. They may have just the right tone of voice, personal mannerisms, and charisma to keep the audience engaged. But even these presenters are more effective when they add visual aids.

Benefit 4: Visual aids help increase retention. Although each of us has a preferred learning style, visual aids do help with the ability of the audience to retain the information they listen to. There have been many publications over the years that refer to the percentage of information audiences retain based on what they read, hear, see, and do. Many people have created visuals which illustrates Dale's Cone of Experience, developed in 1946 by Edgar Dale. The original model, shown in Figure 4.1, provided an intuitive model of various audiovisual media. In Dale's original work, he did not include any numbers or percentages and warned readers not to take the model too literally. Even the final edition of Dale's book, *Dale's Cone of Experience*, published in 1946, did not include any numbers. Over time percentages were added to the illustrations, and soon, like any invalidated data that get published, they became accepted as truth and found their way in many articles and publications.

The percentages and the plot specifically have been passed around in the field from person to person for many years. People have changed the relative percentages and incorrectly cited sources for the numbers. What the cone of influence does suggest is that concept development can proceed from experiences with any specific instructional material. The more numerous and varied the media we employ during our presentations, the richer and more secure will be the concepts we describe. Since each of us has a preferred learning style, the percentages can vary from person to person and using one set of numbers for everyone is not appropriate. Your audience thinks more quickly than you speak, so their minds tend to wander during a presentation. Visual aids help keep your audience focused on your message. Visual aids also add variety and interest to the presentation.

Some people are visual learners, some people are auditory learners, and others are kinesthetic learners. You can be a more effective presenter if you can appeal to all learning styles of your listeners. I will be discussing learning styles in greater detail in Chapter 5.

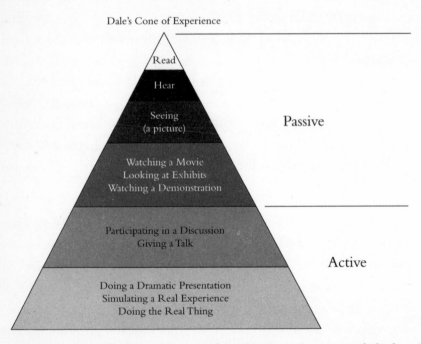

Figure 4.1   Dale's Cone of Influence is a model that incorporates several theories related to instructional design and the learning process.

Benefit 5: Using visual aids help control the presenter's nervousness. Using visual aids give you purposeful physical activity and movement that lets your body process nervous energy without distracting the audience. When using a visual aid, always introduce it before you show it.

TYPES OF VISUAL AIDS

As a presenter you have many types of visual aids available for use during your presentations. Depending on your presentation and what you are trying to accomplish, the type of visual aid you use can make a huge difference. There may be times when having an actual model or prop available is much more effective than showing a photograph.

On the following pages, I will discuss some of the more common types of visual aids along with their advantages and limitations. In addition, I have provided some specific tips on how to use each type of visual aid effectively.

Flip Charts

Flip charts, although not used as much today, still offer a simple and effective method to present information for small groups. Flip charts are very economical, are reusable, and do not require any electricity. Flip charts allow you to add color and spontaneity to your presentation. In our computer-loving world, flip charts may seem pretty low tech, but they are reliable and do not require any special skill to use. Flip charts are usually sold in packages of two and come with or without grids. I personally like those with grids because it makes it easier for me to print straight and I can use the grids to draw or sketch.

I still use flip charts in my presentation skills classes today. By having the participants in my class use flip charts during their presentations, it forces them to think about certain presentation skills concepts they forget when using PowerPoint.

Limitations

Flip charts are generally very large and are difficult to transport. They do have special easel cases you can use to carry them. If your flip charts are too small, they can cause visibility problems. Flip chart paper is often flimsy, and if it is too thin, there can be "see-through" distractions. Flip charts require notable preparation time.

Tips

Following are some specific tips and recommendations for using flip charts:

- Use only a few well-done charts.
- Make your charts simple and bold.
- Keep drawings basic. (Books are available that teach you flip chart drawing.)
- Practice on regular paper before drawing on the actual flip chart pad.
- Use flip chart markers designed for flip charts. Do not use whiteboard markers or permanent markers. Whiteboard markers do not write well on paper, and permanent makers bleed through the flip chart paper.
- When writing on the flip chart pad, first use pencil, then use flip chart markers.
- Use keyword phrases only. It is not necessary to use full sentences.
- Do not capitalize every letter. This makes is difficult to read.

- Add color, particularly dark colors such as blue and black. Avoid using yellow, pink, and orange. These colors are very difficult for the audience to see. Using one color and one accent color works best.

- You can lightly pencil in notes you need right on the flip charts. The audience won't be able to see them. One example of a note you might include is what is on the next flip chart.

- Have a blank sheet of flip chart paper between each of your sheets. This will prevent the written information on the sheets that follow from "peeking through" the flip chart paper.

- Make sure the flip chart pad type you have fits the flip chart stand you will be using. The best type of flip chart stands have clamps at the top of the stand and work with any type of flip chart pad.

- Try to get flip chart pads that have a perforation at the top of the pad. This will allow you to easily remove any sheets as required.

- Many of the flip chart pads today also have nonstick glue on the back of each sheet near the top of the pad. This allows you to remove any sheets and tack them onto a wall.

- Do not talk as you write on the chart. You should always face the audience when talking.

- Properly store and transport your flip charts in a case or the box they came in to protect them from damage.

Making "prepared" flip charts can take a considerable amount of time. Make sure you start preparing your charts early enough that you have time to review them and make any changes or corrections before you actually use them. It takes practice to learn how to print neatly. If you do not have neat printing, ask someone who does print well to prepare them for you. A poorly prepared flip chart can be very distracting.

Overhead Transparencies

Overhead transparencies, although not used as much today, do still exist in many training classrooms. Most facilities still have overhead projectors in training rooms and classrooms. The overhead transparency can be used in a room with normal lighting, and this will increase audience attention and participation. The presenter can face the audience and observe the reactions during the presentation.

Overhead transparencies can be prepared quickly with easy-to-use material and readily available reproduction equipment. You can even buy special transparency sheet films that will allow you to print directly to them from your printer. There are different transparency films to use in your copier machine because the copy machine generates heat and can result in melting your other film types. Make sure you use the correct film type.

Limitations

Awkward changing of overhead transparencies can cause distractions. For the proper use of an overhead projector, an electrical outlet, a screen, and a table or stand are needed. For proper placement of the projector, sufficient space between the overhead projector and the screen must be allocated. Overhead transparencies are not appropriate for small audiences. Their use could seem like overkill. Transparencies get a lot of use and a lot of abuse.

Tips

Following are some specific tips and recommendations for using overhead transparencies:

- To avoid confusion, limit each transparency to one topic or concept.

- Have no more than seven words on a line of text; include no more than six or seven lines of text per transparency.

- Transparencies do not replace the presentation; include a few keywords or ideas.

- If you use transparency frames, you can write notes on the borders.

- Jot down notes on your own paper copies.

- Add color whenever possible.

- Make static transparencies more dynamic by using overlays.

- Choose landscape rather than portrait mode when designing transparency.

- Use a type size of at least 18 points. Figure 4.2 shows the minimum type size you should use based on viewing distance.

- Include illustrations, cartoons, and graphs whenever possible. Remember, however, that the subject matter must be important enough to merit charting in the first place.

- Use tinted transparencies to reduce the lamp glare and to make it easier on the audience's eyes.

- Allow sufficient margins on the visual so that there is room for mounting.

- Number all your transparencies and mount them in frames. This will help in many respects. If you drop them, it will be

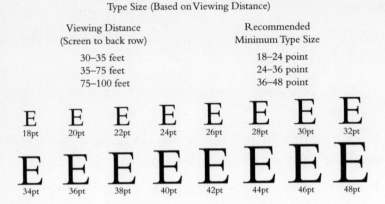

Type Size (Based on Viewing Distance)	
Viewing Distance (Screen to back row)	Recommended Minimum Type Size
30–35 feet	18–24 point
35–75 feet	24–36 point
75–100 feet	36–48 point

Figure 4.2 Font size recommendations based on distance from audience.

easy to rearrange them in order. The frames eliminate the surrounding distracting white space. The frame will also prevent the overhead from sliding due to static buildup. Using frames also provides you somewhere to write some helpful notes about the current slide or what is on the next slide.

- When you need to make last-minute freehand overhead transparencies, place a piece of lined paper under a write-on transparency film. Use special overhead projector pens to write with. Regular marker pens do not write well on transparency films.

- Practice giving your presentation using your actual visual aids. Make sure they project well. Have a friend or colleague sit and watch your presentation and note any problems with your overheads. It takes practice to be able to change overheads smoothly.

- Practice on-site again just before your presentation.

- Make sure all equipment works and always make sure there is an extra bulb. Know how to change the bulb if you need to. Bring a small washcloth or towel to handle the hot bulb if you need to change it. Unplug the projector when changing the bulb.

- Stand off to one side of the projector. Too many speakers stand between the projector and the screen, causing a shadow. Instead, position yourself to allow the audience to see you well, without blocking their view of the overhead.

- Do not face the projected image on the screen. Face and talk to the audience.

- Explain every visual. Use a pointer for complex visuals.

- Never show a blank screen.

Whiteboards, Chalkboards

Most conference rooms have some kind of wall board, such as a chalkboard or whiteboard available to use for your presentation. Using a whiteboard or chalkboard allows your presentation to be very spontaneous and immediate. They are the most flexible visual aid tool because they allow you to easily modify, add, or subtract information. They are readily available and very inexpensive.

Limitations

Legibility can be a problem, especially if you do not draw or write neatly under pressure. It is not always possible to ensure visibility from all parts of the room. The visuals are also temporary and static. Writing and creating your visual aid takes up much of the overall presentation time.

Tips

Following are some specific tips and recommendations for using a whiteboard or chalkboard:

- Practice your handwriting and/or drawing in advance.
- Make sure you draw simply and neatly. People do not expect an artist.
- When writing, use large and legible letters.
- Show only the main points.
- Distinguish between ideas by using a bulleted format.
- Erase any previous visual.
- Keep the presentation flowing and avoid talking to the visual.

Handouts

Most business conferences and meetings involve the use of handouts. When people attend a presentation, they feel cheated if they do not receive a handout. The advantage of providing a handout is that is ensures everyone can see your main points and ideas. Handouts also serve as a reference for later hands–on study. They are economical and facilitate interaction between the presenter and the audience.

Limitations

Handouts can be a distraction during your presentation if they are handed out too early. Often, the audience is reading during your presentation and may even skip ahead of where you are. Color handouts can be expensive, but they are more common today than just a few years ago. If your audience is large, it is difficult to know exactly how many copies of the handout to have.

Tips

Following are some specific tips and recommendations for using handouts:

- Handouts call for more detail than do overhead transparencies or charts.

- Make sure your handouts can stand alone and still make sense several days or weeks after the presentation.

- Some people provide exact copies of the slides they use; take the time to provide more information in you handouts.

- More and more today, people are making their handouts online. Provide the audience with a link to your handout or slides; they will appreciate it. Many of the larger conferences and conventions I speak at no longer provide hardcopy handouts. They provide only a link to download a copy of the material. This saves the organizer and client time and money.

- At a minimum, provide your audience with a copy of the agenda. This allows them to easily follow along.

Photographs or Posters

There are times when the use of photographs or poster offers the best solution to presenting information. I work with many clients, such as architects, military personnel, consultants, and designers, for whom the best visual aid is a large photograph or poster board. This option can often have a bigger impact on your audience than other types of visual aids.

Limitations

Because photos can be small, it is best if the photos are enlarged for your audience to ensure everyone can see the visual. Reproducing large photographs or poster boards, although much easier today, does require time, special equipment, and money. You also do need to have a portfolio case to carry and protect the posters.

Tips

Following are some specific tips and recommendations for using photographs or posters:

- Be certain the quality of the poster or photograph is good.
- Do not use small photos (e.g., traditional 4 × 6 images) for a large group.
- If you have several posters or photos, consider using a slightly smaller size, which will work in most cases.
- Bring along or obtain a few easel boards to display the photos

Videos/Movies/Music

There are times when a video is the best visual you can use for your presentation. Videos or movies can engage the audience's senses more effectively than some other visuals. You can use videos to capture live events that can then be used to make your point. Videos can also serve as a great learning tool. In my presentation skills workshops, I videotape each of the participants' presentations and play them back during my workshop. I used to use a VHS recorder to tape the participants. In order to play these back, I need to have a VCR player and a monitor. I used this technology for several years.

I began using digital video cameras when they came out, and this allowed me to use a smaller video camera, making it more portable. I was then able to play the video back through my liquid crystal display (LCD) projector. This was a great improvement since the large VCR camera and large TV monitor was no longer required.

I now currently use a Flip camera and play the recorded videos back directly through my laptop computer. Fortunately, LCD projectors also have gotten smaller, lighter, and more durable, making it easier for me to travel with this equipment. I no longer have to rent or make special arrangements for this equipment. The Flip camera is very small and portable and is about the size of your cell phone or smartphone.

Limitations

I often see other trainers and speakers, including professional speakers, use personal copies of commercial tapes or DVDs such as movies or documentaries in their presentations or training classes. A word of caution here: Videos purchased for personal use can be used *only* for personal home viewing and use. You are not legally allowed to use these videos—even short clips—in your presentations or classroom without written permission from the author or copyright holder. Re-read the legal statements on the videos.

I have seen too many people use a personal copy of a commercial video during presentations. Many people think that just because they purchased and own a copy of the video, they can now legally play this video in a public forum. These videos are for personal home viewing only. You need to obtain written permission to use them in a public presentation.

The same applies to presenters using commercial cartoons, such as Dilbert and others, within their presentations. This is illegal unless the appropriate licensing fees have been paid and written permission obtained. Companies have been sued and have been required to pay millions of dollars in fines for violating these copyright and performance right laws.

The use of commercial music, whether in a training class, workshop, or seminar—and even if played only during a break—also requires licensing. Even hotels must pay a licensing fee from ASCAP and others to play music from the local radio station through their intercom system. Having music at breaks and other times can help and add to the atmosphere of your program; however, you can get yourself in serious legal trouble if you do not know the law.

You can purchase royalty-free music for this purpose. I have owned and used royalty-free music for years, and I use this music during breaks and even during exercises to provide a soothing background for my participants.

Make sure you are not violating any of the issues I've described, or you may find yourself on the wrong end of a lawsuit.

Tips

Following are some specific tips and recommendations for using videos, movies, or music:

- Never show a commercial film or video without written permission.
- Never show a film or video you have not previewed.
- If possible, have an assistant help you with the video equipment.
- If you decide to incorporate video clips into your PowerPoint presentation, make sure you know how to

load and start the video and make sure the computer and system you are using is set up for sound.

- Always introduce the video before you use it and explain why you are showing it.

- Pay attention to the room's lighting conditions.

- After watching the film or video, invite a discussion about what was just seen.

- Allow yourself plenty of time to set up your equipment prior to the presentation.

- Check all your cable connections and check the volume on the speakers.

- If you use a camera to record during your program, use a tripod.

Computer LCD Projectors

In today's world of ever-changing technology, the use of PowerPoint and the LCD projector is commonplace. They are more common today due to the drastically reduced prices of this high-tech equipment. When LCD projectors first came out, they were very large, very heavy, and very, very expensive. Many of the first-generation projectors weighed more than 20 pounds and required a special travel case because the LCD projector bulb was so fragile—and expensive. When LCD projectors debuted, it was not unusual to have to pay $10,000 to $100,000 for this equipment. The projector bulbs inside typically lasted only a couple hundred hours and cost anywhere from $500 to $1,000 each to replace. The projectors would overheat easily, and the bulbs would burn out.

As technology improved, the projectors became smaller and smaller and the bulbs more durable. They eventually came out with the portable LCD projector that was much smaller, lighter, and more durable. My first LCD projector was an 800-lumens projector (lumens is a measure of the total "amount" of visible light emitted by a source). The projector weighed only six pounds, and the bulb was designed to last about 2,000 hours. When I invested (and believe me it was an investment) in my first portable LCD projector, I spent $3,999. This was a lot of money even by today's standards. But I needed to make this investment because it was costing me even more to rent LCD projectors (many companies and clients did not own their own, so I needed to bring this equipment with me).

Fast-forward to today, where you can purchase a smaller portable LCD projector for less than $800. The LCD projectors today offer much brighter light at a very inexpensive cost. Many of the projectors used today in classrooms are 2,500- to 3,000-lumen projectors. When I first started traveling more internationally, I need to bring my 2,500-lumen LCD projector because they were not readily available in many countries. Many of the LCD projectors today are even wireless, making it possible to connect several input devices at the same time.

Limitations

As with any technology, there is a small learning curve to know how to connect and set these devices to your computer and the devices. If you need sound, then you need to connect the projector to some type of sound system. I travel with my small LCD projector and small set of portable speakers. The portable speakers plug into the USB port of my laptop and allow me to have louder volume than just using my laptop speakers. I project the image onto a movie screen, which is available in most training classrooms.

Tips

Following are some specific tips and recommendations for using computer LCD projectors:

- Familiarize yourself with the proper setup and operation of your equipment.

- The more technology you bring into a presentation, the more care and time you need to properly prepare.

- Read and understand the owner's manual of your LCD equipment.

- Set up your equipment well in advance of your presentation.

- Always check out your equipment beforehand to make sure it is working.

- Understand how to toggle the function keys on your laptop to allow your computer to talk to the LCD projector. Different computer brands use different function keys, so know what you need to do to display your computer image through the LCD projector.

- Check the LCD projector bulb for available life span. Most modern LCD projectors have a menu option that allows you to check this information.

- Become familiar with the LCD projector menu options to ensure you know how to modify your setup. Options vary with each projector.

- Check that the LCD projector is placed or positioned the proper distance from the display screen. This will vary depending on the room size and the size of your audience.

- The larger the audience, the larger the room and the brighter LCD projector needs to be since you need to project the image farther onto a larger screen.

- Check your presentation color combinations. Many color combinations that look good on your laptop screen do not project well on the larger screen.

- Check the font size in your presentation and be sure it is appropriate and projects well. Participants in the back of the room should be able to easily read the text.

MORE ABOUT USING VISUAL AIDS

Regardless of the type of visual aids you use, you need to practice and rehearse using them with your presentation. Do not limit yourself to using only PowerPoint. Be creative and use a variety of props and visual aids during your presentation. If you plan to use a variety of visual aids, be sure to remember to bring them with you the day of your presentation. Make a checklist of the items you need to bring with you. You will be glad you did. I still use checklists today with all my presentations. I make a list of what I need to bring with me. On that same checklist I have a spot or box to check to make sure that I (1) remembered to include that item and (2) I actually packed that item with my equipment in preparations for my travel.

Following are some additional general tips to consider when using visual aids:

- Keep your visual aids simple, serviceable, and easily visible.

- Your visual aid should be an integral part of your subject and needed to support your presentation. Your presentation should be more clearly understood with their inclusion than by words alone.

- The visual aid you use needs to be suited to the subject.

- Talk to the audience *after* you have pointed to the screen or object. Face the audience when you speak and avoid speaking at the screen.

- Become so familiar with your visual aid that you only need to glance at it. There is no need to continually glance back at the same visual aid while you are talking.

- Do not stand in front of or obstruct the view of the visual aid.

- Do not fiddle with the visual aid once you introduce it. Do not continue to hold it in your hands any longer than you need to. Put the visual aid down to free up your hands.

- For optimal visibility, place your screen or flip charts off-center in the room. This allows you to remain on "center stage" and provides a better viewing angle for your audience.

- Use color to emphasize key points, but avoid using too many colors.

- Do not use so many visual aids that they become a crutch. Use them sparingly.

THE MOST IMPORTANT VISUAL AID

With all presentations, you have many options to use a variety of visual aids. The single most important visual aid is you, the presenter. Learn to use your body, gestures, and body language effectively because you are the focus of your presentation. I will be discussing in Chapter 6 more about using yourself as a visual aid when I discuss nonverbal messages.

For now, I will provide some last-minute tips to consider when you are the visual aid:

When You Are the Visual Aid

1. *Do not have a sloppy appearance.* Dress professionally and at least as well as the best dressed member of your audience. The typical business attire today has shifted dramatically since I first started speaking professionally. When I first started providing seminars and workshops to my corporate and association clients, the typical business attire was a sports coat, shirt, and tie for men and dresses or business suits with skirts for women. Most of the business environments I now present in have become very casual. Most of the audience members are wearing golf shirts and slacks. Women are no longer wearing dresses or skirts. They are wearing slacks. This shift has occurred to provide a more comfortable work environment.

   A good part of my business takes me to countries all over the world, and more recently, I have established a presence in the Middle East. My exclusive agent, Medex International, arranges my seminars and workshops in more than 22 countries in the Middle East. When I travel internationally, I am still often required to wear a suit and tie. I provide many programs out of Dubai, UAE, and during my upcoming four-day program in Dubai, I will be wearing a suit every day, all day, during my entire program. This is the expectation of their business climate. When you travel to give a presentation, whether it is locally or internationally, understand what the expectation is for your attire. The same holds true here in the United States. I still wear suits and ties for many of my speaking engagements based on the venue, the client, and my audience. There is no bigger visual aid then yourself. Others will form their first impression of you based on how you are dressed.

2. *Do not burry your hand in your pocket.* Do not play with the change in your pocket or with your jewelry. This is a distraction.

3. *Do not hide behind the lectern.* (Note: A lectern is what you stand behind; a podium is a raised platform you stand on. Many people today mistake the two and often refer to the lectern as a podium.)

4. *Use your hands to describe as much as you can.* Use descriptive gestures. This will be discussed more in Chapter 6.

5. *Always face your audience, not the visual aid, when you speak.* Never turn your back to the audience.

CHAPTER 5

Learning Styles

We all learn through a combination of different learning styles, and over time, we develop our own preferred way of learning. Some of us are visual learners, some of us are auditory learners, and others may prefer a kinesthetic or physical approach to learning. No one style is better than another.

Many people adapt a particular learning style depending on the actual learning situation. How we go about processing information is dictated by this learning style. As a presenter, you need to keep in mind that not all people learn in the same way. Each of the members in your audience may have a different learning style than you do; you need to take these different learning styles into consideration. Although some participants in your audience may prefer to see lots of visual aids, other participants may prefer to just sit back and listen to your presentation. Some participants love to take notes. Others may hate to take notes.

Once you understand your own learning style, you will be able to better prepare your presentations. Since, in most cases, you do not know which preferred learning style your audience uses, you need to consider using as many learning styles during the delivery of your presentation as is feasible.

In this chapter, I discuss the seven most common learning styles:

Seven Learning Styles

1. Visual or spatial
2. Auditory or aural
3. Verbal or linguistic
4. Physical or kinesthetic
5. Logical or mathematical

6. Social or interpersonal

7. Solitary or intrapersonal

Let's take a look at the characteristics of each of these and how to best incorporate each learning style during your presentations.

VISUAL OR SPATIAL

Those who are visual learners prefer to learn by looking at photographs, pictures, videos, charts, graphs, maps, and so on. As a student, I always learned better by watching and observing. I am clearly a visual learner and need to visually see things. I needed to have someone show me a diagram or picture for me to fully understand what was being taught. I did not learn well if the teacher just spoke and did not write notes on the blackboard while presenting. I needed to "see" what was being taught and could not rely just on what was being said. If you ask me to remember a list of items and only list them verbally for me, I usually cannot remember the entire list. On the other hand, if you visually show me that same list and allow me to read it as you read it aloud, I generally can remember the entire list.

If you are attending a workshop or seminar and are a visual learner, you prefer to see the outline of the program before the program begins. You like using color and hope that the workshop provides a handout or workbook so that you can visually follow along with the presenter. As a presenter, you like including many types of images in your presentations.

Characteristics of Visual Learners

- Are very good at spelling because they can visualize the words
- Generally forget names easily

- Prefer to study in quiet settings because noises distract them
- Like to use color
- Understand charts and diagrams better than most people
- Like to use mind maps
- Prefer to see pictures or illustrations instead of text
- Are better at visualizing ideas and concepts

What You Can Provide Visual Learners during Your Presentations

- Provide an agenda of what you will be presenting to them.
- Show them a visual or create a visual of what you are saying.
- Provide them with a means to take notes, such as a handout or workbook.
- Use a variety of visual aids.
- Use a lot of color during your presentation.
- When providing a workshop, use poster boards or flip chart pages you can display.
- Include videos (that you have written permission to use) in your presentation.

AUDITORY OR AURAL

Those who learn best by hearing things, who like to work with sound and music, and who have a good sense of pitch and rhythm are probably auditory learners. They typically can carry a tune when singing, probably play a musical instrument, and like to hum or sing music.

My oldest son, Michael, is an auditory learner. Michael, now married with three children, has an amazing ability to listen to a movie or play and recall details with uncanny accuracy. When Michael was a student, I remember helping him study for school quizzes and tests. He would have me read material to him and then quiz him later. He needed to listen and hear me describe the materials in the chapter he was studying. Michael was not a visual learner and did not like to read.

Characteristics of Auditory Learners

- Like to read out loud to themselves so they can hear what they are reading
- Prefer to take oral tests instead of written tests
- Remember names easily
- Enjoy listening to music
- Are generally slow readers and prefer to listen to audiobooks
- Learn foreign languages easily by listening to audio recordings
- Follow spoken directions well
- Work well in study groups where ideas are shared verbally
- Are very willing to speak up in class
- Explain things well to other people

What You Can Provide Auditory Learners during Your Presentations

- Include time for group discussions as part of your presentation.
- Provide a recording of your presentation.

- Use videos during your presentation.
- Use audio recordings during your presentation.
- Allow them to record your presentation.

VERBAL OR LINGUISTIC

Verbal or linguistic learners rely on the written and spoken word to learn. Verbal learners usually need to talk things out and repeat things to themselves.

Characteristics of Verbal Learners

- Need to talk it out
- Need to hear themselves talk
- Love to participate in brainstorming sessions
- Express themselves well
- Learn best when taught using spoken word or written materials
- Prefer math word problems to solving equations
- Typically enjoy written projects
- Like debates
- Are usually good at journalism

What You Can Provide Verbal Learners during Your Presentations

- Provide them with reading activities.
- Provide them with writing activities.
- Include activities based on language reasoning.
- If applicable, include math word problems.

- Include tongue twisters, rhymes, and limericks.
- Provide a pneumonic or acronym for remembering material.
- Offer role-playing exercises.

PHYSICAL OR KINESTHETIC

Kinesthetic learners lean best by doing things. They need to experience the activity directly. Kinesthetic learners are not afraid to get their hands dirty. They are more inclined to use gestures and body language. When you present to these learners, you want to use very descriptive gestures such that you help paint a picture in the audience's mind. They learn best by role-playing and physically simulating a given situation.

Characteristics of Kinesthetic Learners

- Do not mind getting up and dancing
- Prefer to "jump in" as soon as possible
- Prefer to participate in hands-on activities
- Like to physically touch objects such a props
- Like to role-play
- Like to simulate situations
- Love using flash cards

What You Can Provide Kinesthetic Learners during Your Presentations

- Provide them with reading activities.
- Provide them with activities that involve touch, action, and movement.

- Include verbal descriptions of the physical feelings (e.g., "I felt the wind blow through my hair as I sped down the road").
- Ask them to write things out, such as making lists.
- Ask them to draw or illustrate using drawings.
- Use breathing and relaxation exercises.
- Use role-playing exercises.
- Use demonstration techniques.

LOGICAL OR MATHEMATICAL

Logical learners use their brains for logical and mathematical reasoning. Logical learners recognize patterns easily and are able to group and classify information as needed to better understand it.

Characteristics of Logical Learners

- Easily recognize patterns
- Work well with numbers
- Can perform complex calculations
- Can easily do math in their heads
- Work through problems systematically
- Set goals and dates and track their progress
- Like creating agendas, itineraries, and to-do lists
- Support their points with examples or statistics
- Like working out strategies and using simulations
- Look for logical associations between items.

What You Can Provide Logical Learners during Your Presentations

- Provide games or thinking activities during your program.
- Include lists.
- Include key points in your presentation.
- Use system diagrams to show how things fit together.
- Be very organized.
- Recommend solutions that are methodical.

SOCIAL OR INTERPERSONAL

Social learners communicate very well with people. They are usually looked at people to seek advice from. They listen well and make a point to understand others. They make good mentors.

Characteristics of Social Learners

- Typically stay around after class to talk with others
- Prefer social activities instead of being alone
- Like attending sports activities
- Listen well
- Take the time to understand people
- Enjoy mentoring others

What You Can Provide Social Learners during Your Presentations

- Provide activities that require people to work together.
- Include role-playing opportunities.

- Provide opportunities for participants to share their thinking and approach with others.
- Agree to disagree.
- Use mind maps and diagrams.

SOLITARY OR INTRAPERSONAL

Solitary learners are very introspective people. They like working alone and being independent. Solitary people like to spend time alone and tend to stay away from crowds. They like being in remote places and like to feel independent. They know what they want.

Characteristics of Solitary Learners

- Like working alone and being independent
- Usually avoid crowds
- Like attending self-help seminars and workshops
- Have read all the self-help books
- Prefer to work on problems by going somewhere quiet to work
- Tend to spend too much time trying to solve the problem
- Like making plans
- Like setting goals
- Know what they want to do with their lives
- Feel a need to always know their direction in life
- Always request time to think things over
- Like to think about things that will get back to people

What You Can Provide Solitary Learners during Your Presentations

- Provide activities that require people to work together.
- Allow these types of people to work alone when you can.
- Allow time for participants to make their own personal lists before asking them to share.
- Provide role-play exercises for your participants.

MIXED LEARNING STYLES

As a presenter, you will now always know what the preferred learning style will be of the people in your audience. The makeup of your audience will be a mixture and variety of learning styles; your challenge as a presenter is to design and deliver your presentation to reach all of these leaner types at the same time. You must think about how you will be presenting your material and try to use as many learning styles as you can at the same time.

PRESENTATION ENVIRONMENT

As varied as each of these learners are, they also have their own preferences regarding the presentation environment. Several environmental factors also influence your audiences and need to be considered. Following are some tips and advice to factor into your presentation and workshops when designing and developing your presentations.

Formal versus Informal Setting

A formal setting may include a classroom, an auditorium, or even a table. An informal setting would be the floor, couch, or outside on a blanket. I remember when I was in college, one of my professors held his classes outside. We were asked to bring a blanket and sunglasses so we would be comfortable. At first we all thought this was strange, but soon we looked forward to this class each week. None of the students ever skipped this class, and we did actually learn a lot.

Noise versus Quiet

Some people cannot learn or study in complete silence. Others are the opposite and cannot learn or study when there are too many distractions. Noise can be calming to some and an annoyance to others. I am the type of person who could not study unless I had some kind of background noise, such as music playing, while I was studying. My wife, on the other hand, prefers total quiet and is easily distracted by sounds and conversations.

Temperature

The temperature of the room you speak and present in has a huge impact on the learning process. If participants are too cold or too hot, they will have a difficult time staying focused on what you are saying. It is better to have a room on the cooler side than one that is too warm. If a room is too warm, people have a tendency to drift asleep. In a cooler room, some people will be very comfortable and those who are cool can easily put on a jacket or sweater (assuming they remembered to bring one with them).

Several years ago I was hired to provide a series of workshops for a client in six major cities around the United States. One of the cities was Chicago. The two-day program was being held at my client's Chicago office during the third week in October. Their company was one of several companies that rented space in this large office building. When I arrived at their office in the morning, it was 35 degrees outside. The temperature of the conference room I was scheduled to use over the next two days was 53 degrees. This was very cold for anyone to work in for two days. I knew that some large office buildings turn their heat off during the weekend to save money and that the heat is usually turned back on first thing Monday morning. I initially assumed this was the case. I asked if there was any way we could turn the heat back on. The person put in charge to help me set up for my program told me he could not do anything about the heat since the heat in the entire building was not turned on until November 1. The owner of the building did this to save money, and seeing that most of the office tenants were sales companies, they usually were not in the building every day anyway. Myself, along with the 16 participants in my sales presentations class, had to suffer with this cold room for two days and there was nothing I or anyone there could do about it.

I had a similar situation where I was speaking to more than 1,000 people in a large college auditorium that was very, very warm. The air-conditioning was broken or being worked on, and we had to sit in a room that was about 85 degrees. As a presenter, you may be faced with similar situations. You need to be able to adapt your delivery style to allow for these extreme temperature conditions.

Bright versus Dim Lighting

The lighting in the room you present in can make it difficult for your audience. The room should be bright enough for people to see you but not so bright that it is distracting to your audience.

Comfort of the Seats

There is nothing worse than to have to sit in an uncomfortable chair or seat for a long time. Also, people cannot sit still for long periods of time without feeling the need to stand up and stretch. Be sure to take short breaks to allow people to move around. I never speak for more than 45 minutes without allowing my audience to take a stretch break. Some people's bladders will also appreciate you allowing them to take a break to stop at the rest room.

MYERS-BRIGGS

Many studies have looked at how best to account for the various learning styles in teaching and presentations. As discussed in the previous section, we now understand that each of us has a preferred learning style. As a presenter, you do not know what learning style each of the participants who attend your program prefers. This means that as a presenter it is your responsibility to use a variety of learning techniques during your presentations to ensure that you engage all the participants.

When you present on a topic you are passionate about, it is easy to forget how the information you present is being received. You can get so caught up in trying to cover all the planned content that you sometimes forget to deliver this information using a variety of presentation styles. The preferred learning style of individual participants in your audience will greatly influence how much information each person retains. In order to better understand learning styles, you should take a look at Myers–Briggs Type Indicator.

The Myers–Briggs Type Indicator was developed by Isabel Briggs Myers and Katherine Cooks Briggs. An individual's personality profile is identified along four dimensions:

- Orientation to life (Extroverted/Introverted)
- Perception (Sensing/Intuitive)

- Decision Making (Thinking/Feeling)
- Attitude toward the outside world (Judgment/Perception)

People are said to belong to 1 of 16 categories, based on their preferences along each of these dimensions. An introverted, sensing, feeling, and judging person would then be categorized as having an ISFJ personality. An extraverted, intuitive, thinking, and judging person would be categorized as having an ENTJ personality, and so on.

What does this mean for you as a presenter? You cannot be expected to develop a different presentation style for each personality type; however, you should strive to use and incorporate a variety of learning styles during your presentations. It is your responsibility to take this into consideration when developing your presentation. The presenter who does this effectively will be better received by the entire audience.

CHAPTER 6

Nonverbal Messages

Research has demonstrated that more than half of all human communication takes place on the nonverbal level. When you present in front of an audience, your audience will base their judgment of you and your message on what they see as well as what they hear.

Your body can be a very effective tool for adding emphasis and clarity to your words. Your nonverbal message is your most powerful instrument for convincing your audience of your sincerity, earnestness, and enthusiasm. Keep in mind that if your physical actions do not agree with your verbal message, your body can defeat your words. Effective speech delivery involves the whole person.

GESTURES—LET YOUR BODY SPEAK

Effective presentation delivery involves the whole person. You need to learn to use your entire body as an instrument of communication. You, the speaker or presenter, are the most important visual aid of all. Following are some good reasons to use yourself as a visual aid.

1. You do not have to darken the room to be seen. In the old days, the technology was limited to 35-mm slides or using an overhead projector. Due to the technology, it was necessary to lower or reduce the room lighting to be able to see any projected image. When you lowered the lights, it then became very difficult to see the speaker.

2. You do not burn out. Unlike overhead projectors and other equipment, there is no special lightbulb that can burn out and need to be replaced.

3. You yourself do not need electricity. There is no need to look for somewhere to plug yourself in.

4. Like a slide projector, you do not jam up.

5. You do not break.

6. You aren't one dimensional.

7. You do not need a special technician to operate you.

When You Are the Visual Aid

Because you will be the focus of attention when using your body as a visual aid, there are some considerations you need to be aware of:

1. *Do not have a sloppy appearance when you are presenting.* You should always dress at least as well as the best dressed member of your audience. There are speaking situations where I am able to dress casually and wear slacks and a golf shirt. Other times, such as when I am in Dubai, UAE, the accepted business culture expects the presenter to wear a professional-looking business suit.

2. *Do not bury your hands in your pocket.* Later in this chapter, when I talk about resting positions, I will discuss what to do with your hands.

3. *Do not play with your jewelry or with any change that's in your pocket.* Better yet, do not carry any change in your pockets at all. Many speakers find themselves fidgeting and look to do something with their hands.

4. *Do not hide behind the lectern.* This creates a barrier between you and the audience. Move out from behind the lectern.

5. *Do use your hands (gesture) to describe as much as you can.*

6. *Always face the audience when you are speaking and do not face and stare at the screen.* You should never turn your back to the audience.

Presenters who learn to use themselves as a visual aid will be more effective than those who do not. When you present, your audience judges not only your presentation but also you. If your audience is convinced about your earnestness and sincerity, they are most likely to accept your spoken message. Who you are is more clearly communicated through your nonverbal behavior than through your words.

When you deliver your presentation, your listeners will use all of their senses and watch you as you speak. They will determine whether:

- You are sincere.
- You welcome the opportunity to speak.
- You truly believe what you are saying.
- You are interested in them and care about them.
- You are confident and in control.

Your physical actions speak louder than your actual words. Let's consider the following example.

The Nervous Speaker

Shuffling his notes, a man staggers to the lectern. He clears his throat, grabs the lectern tightly and plunges into his presentation by saying, "It's a great pleasure to be here today. I have a message of extreme importance to you."

The effect of these opening remarks was anything but positive. Although his words expressed pleasure in addressing his audience, he transmitted a clearly contradictory nonverbal message: "I'm in terrible pain. I do not want to be anywhere near here."

These visual messages were generated by simple nervousness and inexperience and were transmitted unconsciously. Such nonverbal communication branded the speaker as insincere, indifferent, and incompetent, even though he was none of these things.

When you speak, your audience will tend to mirror your attitudes as they perceive them through their senses. It is vital, therefore, that your body faithfully portray your true feelings. If you appear nervous, your audience will probably be nervous. If you fidget, they will perceive a lack of self-control in you.

Benefits of Effective Physical Action

Providing a true barometer of your feelings and attitudes is the single greatest benefit of purposeful, effective physical action in delivering presentations. There are other benefits was well:

1. *Physical actions make messages more meaningful.* People tend to become bored with things that do not move. They find it hard to resist the temptation to look at moving objects. In addition, audiences will remember messages that reach multiple senses; therefore, gestures, body movements, and facial expressions can be valuable tools when employed skillfully.

2. *Physical actions add punctuation to your presentations.* Written language includes an array of symbols for punctuating messages: commas, periods, exclamation points, and so on. When you speak, you use an entirely different set of

symbols to show what part of your speech is most important and to add power and vitality to your words. To best achieve your goals, you need to coordinate your voice with your body, making them work together.

3. *Physical actions help relieve nervous tension.* Being nervous before a presentation is actually healthy and normal. It shows that your presentation is important to you. Fear and nervousness in public speaking work on three levels:

- Mental level
- Emotional level
- Physical level

I have had a survey on my website for several years, and the survey asks only one question. How comfortable are you speaking in front of an audience? I give you a choice of four possible answers: very uncomfortable, slightly uncomfortable, comfortable, and very comfortable. More than 15,000 people took the time to take this short survey. I did not ask for any information about the person taking it. The responder was required only to answer this one question. Following is the breakdown of responses to this question.

How comfortable are you speaking in front of an audience?

Very uncomfortable	54 percent
Uncomfortable	27 percent
Comfortable	10 percent
Very comfortable	9 percent
Total	**100 percent**

You can see from the response that 81 percent of the responders said they were either very uncomfortable or uncomfortable. This says that more than 8 out of 10 responders fell into one of these categories. If you are one of those eight people, do not feel alone. You are in the majority. Being in the majority indicates that this response is normal and there is nothing wrong with that. Many of the participants in my seminars and workshops who indicate they are very nervous believe they are the only ones who feel this way. During the workshop they are very surprised to find out that most everyone else in that same workshop also has the same feeling of high speaking anxiety.

For those of you who are very uncomfortable, you may be surprised to know that many successful and experienced people all experienced high speaking anxiety. This includes people such as Franklin Roosevelt, Ronald Regan, Billy Graham, Jane Fonda, Barbra Streisand, and several others. All of these people, just like many of you, have admitted to extremely high levels of speaking anxiety.

PERFORMANCE ORIENTATION VERSUS CONVERSATIONAL MODE

In Chapter 2 I talked about some of the techniques you can use to reduce this speaking anxiety. I provided some physical and mental techniques you could use to avoid looking nervous. If I were to ask the 81 percent of my survey responders what symptoms they experience, they would most likely all list the same one. The physical and mental symptoms, along with their fear interpretation, combine to start a vicious cycle. When any of us experiences fear, regardless of whether or not these fears are of real or perceived threats, our minds and our bodies react to them in the same way. That is, our bodies begin to respond physiologically in the same way, and we begin to experience many of the same symptoms.

Extremely nervous speakers interpret these symptoms as being valid and begin to look for reasons why these feelings are justified. They say to themselves, "You see, I knew I would get nervous." This self-justification further amplifies the symptoms, and the fears get worse and more intense. They then begin to worry about what the audience is thinking about them and focus on themselves and worry about their gestures, their language, their eye contact, and how they appear to the audience. They begin to look for additional reasons why they should feel this anxiety and develop an incorrect view of delivering a presentation and think of them more as a performance. Zig Ziglar, a famous professional speaker, says the word *fear* stands for "false evidence appearing real." In the case of the high-anxiety speaker, it stands for "forget everything and run."

You have to ask yourself, "What starts this process and vicious cycle of nervousness?" High-anxiety speakers approach public speaking and delivering presentations as a formal situation and as a performance. They falsely think that the audience is also looking at them and severely judging them and their performance. They feel they need to be perfect and cannot make any mistakes.

For the participants in my presentation skills programs, I ask that they approach their presentations as simply a conversation with an audience. Each of you carry on conversations every day with your friends, colleagues, and people you just met. When you run into a friend you have not seen for a while, you strike up a conversation and begin to talk for several minutes about what you have been doing. While you are talking, you are also using natural gestures and not giving it any thought as to what the other person is thinking about you. You are merely having a conversation.

When you are in performance mode, you feel you are being evaluated and start to worry about what you are saying and how you are saying it. In conversational mode, you do not do this.

This performance mode triggers your body's reaction and triggers your fear. For many of you, this trigger point may occur hours, days, or even weeks before your presentation. I have been providing presentation skills programs for many years, and whenever someone in the class tells me he or she is one of these extremely high-anxiety speakers, I usually cannot wait to see that person present. When I, along with the other participants, watch this person present, we are pleasantly surprised and in some cases shocked to see how well the person looked and presented. When the speaker hears that he or she did not look nervous—even when the entire class gives that feedback—that person often does not believe it. When I play the video of the presentation for the speaker, he or she is also pleasantly surprised at how relaxed he or she looked, especially knowing the anxiety that was present during the presentation. It is a real plus for speakers to be able to watch themselves present and see proof that they didn't look as nervous as they felt on the inside. Because of their high anxiety, many speakers at my workshops have no desire to present in front of a video camera, as I require them to do in my presentation skills class. But watching their videos gives them a new perspective on how they truly look while presenting. Over the course of my workshop, they are recorded several times. They get to watch these videos and eventually start to realize that their perception before was unfounded.

I work with these participants in my class to prepare and deliver their presentations using conversational language and phrases. Many presenters try to memorize what they have on their slides. What's worse, the language or phrases they put on their slides is not conversational style language.

When asked what is the one piece of advice I can share to help reduce performance anxiety, I tell them they need to approach preparing and delivering presentations as a conversation. They need to focus on simply having a conversation with their audience using conversational language. This is key. What you need to do is to first use very little text on your visual aids. The more text you place on your visual, the more you will have a tendency to read the text on your visual aid. Instead, use short conversational phrases (they do not have to be complete sentences). This does a couple of things for you.

1. It allows you to quickly see and capture the short phrase in your mind.

2. It then allows you to conversationally state what you want to say using this short phrase as an aid to what you need to say. It is not important that you worry about the exact words before you say them. Just say the words in a conversational sentence using your own natural conversational style.

Too many presenters, when preparing their visual aids, write out complete sentences because they want to make sure they do not forget something. The problem with this is that you end up reading that entire text on the visual aid when you present because you feel you need to do so to sound perfect. Furthermore, you will have a tendency to use your written style instead of your speaking, conversation style. For most people, this is completely different. The sooner you can learn to write like you speak and do so in a conversational manner, the easier this process becomes. Also, by limiting the amount of text on your slides, you avoid staring at the visual while you talk. When there is too much text on your visual aid, you are almost forced to keep looking back at it to avoid losing your place.

Once you have modified your visual aid to have only simple phrases or even have a picture, you will find yourself speaking more conversationally. Not relying on too much text will actually make it less restrictive to you and what you are going to say. You may see this slide several times, and each time say it slightly differently. That's okay. Do not get hung up thinking that you need to say it the same every time. Some people feel the need to memorize what they want to say, but this is the worst thing you can do.

Once you begin to use conversational language and a conversational delivery, you will begin to use more natural gestures. Using this conversational approach will greatly improve your speaking as a presenter. Performance-oriented speakers, on the other hand, are so focused on saying the right words, using the right gestures, and using the right vocal inflection that they get caught up in trying to analyze their presentations while they are presenting. When they do this, they are not focusing on communicating their message conversationally. Think about it. When you run into a friend you have not seen in a while and strike up a conversation, you just have a conversation. You are not saying to yourself, "Do this with my hand, stand here while I talk, and say this and say that." You just have a conversation.

As a presenter, you need to use this same approach and focus on using your natural speaking style to have a conversation with your audience. You need to adapt the same one-on-one conversational style you use when talking to a friend and bring that same style to your presentations.

Think about this for a second. If, after not having seen you for a long time, I ran into you on the street and asked you to tell me what you do for a living, you would conversationally describe what you do. If instead, I asked you during one of my presentation classes the same question when you first arrived in the workshop room, again you would probably say the same general thing but not using the exact same words. If later that morning, I asked you to stand up in front of the class and share with us what you do for a living, you would have a tendency to go into performance mode—simply because you stood up in front of a group of people. Do not do this.

Just stand up and speak to the audience in the exact manner you did when you spoke to me on the street or when you walked in the classroom. Have a conversation with the audience. The sooner you can approach your presentation using this conversational style, the sooner you will see your anxiety reduce—and your presentations will automatically improve.

Improve with Experience

You will find that the more you present and the more experience you gain, the easier this will become. Experienced speakers generally have lower anxiety than speakers with less experience. To gain experience you need to speak. High-anxiety presenters tend to avoid giving presentations and thus do not give themselves the experience they need to improve. These high-anxiety speakers avoid, at all costs, giving presentations. The sooner you actually get up and speak, the sooner this will change.

Your Speaking Posture and Gestures

A common question from nervous presenters is, "What do I do with my stupid hands?" How you position your body when you speak communicates a set of visual messages to an audience. Good posture also helps presenters breathe properly and project their voice more effectively. In this next section, I am going to discuss the use of gestures and how to use your hands effectively.

Gestures are specific body movements that should be used to reinforce your verbal message. Most gestures are made using your hands and arms. Your hands can be a marvelous tool for communication. Your gestures can suggest a very precise meaning to an audience. To be an effective presenter, your gestures need to be purposeful. They must have the same meaning to the audience as they do to you, the presenter. Gestures are used to reflect not only what is being said, but the total personality behind the message. No other kind of physical action can enhance your presentations in as many ways as gestures. Let's look at some of the key attributes about gestures:

- *Gestures clarify and support your words.* They strengthen the audience's understanding of your verbal message.
- *Gestures dramatize your ideas.* They help paint vivid pictures in your listeners' minds.
- *Gestures lend emphasis and vitality.* They help you convey your feelings and your attitudes.
- *Gestures help dissipate nervous tension.* They are a good outlet for nervous energy. Using gestures will help dissipate that nervous energy.
- *Gestures function as visual aids.* They enhance audience attentiveness and retention.
- *Gestures stimulate audience participation.* They help elicit the response you want.
- *Gestures are highly visible.* They provide visual support.

TYPES OF GESTURES

Gestures can be grouped into four main categories.

1. *Descriptive gestures:* These are used to describe something. This may include how big something is, how long it is,

how tall it is, how wide it is, how heavy it is, where it is located, what it does, and so on. Descriptive gestures are used the most during a presentation.

Example: Try this for yourself. Stand up and think about how you would describe, using your hands, something that is tiny. Now describe something that looks round. What did you do with your hands? Initially you had to think because I asked you to describe some specific things. Using your hands and your body, how would you show something that is underneath, something that is next to you, something that is off in the distance? Notice what you are doing with your hands. A descriptive gesture is best used for these types of examples.

2. *Emphatic gestures:* These gestures underscore what is being said (e.g., a clenched fist suggests strong feelings, such as anger or determination).

    Example: Think about when you watch Tiger Woods sink that 20-foot putt and he clenches his fist and shakes his arm with excitement. Remember your excitement when you rolled that strike during a game of bowling. These are emphatic gestures.

3. *Suggestive gestures:* These are symbols of ideas or emotions that suggest some kind of action.

    Example: You extend out your hand with the palm of your hand facing up asking for someone to pass you the pen.

4. *Prompting gestures:* These are used to evoke a desired response from the audience.

    Example: While you are presenting, you raise your hand while asking your audience if they have any questions. By you raising you hand first, you are prompting them to raise their hands.

LOCATIONS OF GESTURES

The location of your gestures can influence the emotion communicated by the actual gesture you use. Gestures, depending on their meaning, have different locations relative to the body.

1. *Gestures above the shoulders* suggest physical height, inspiration, uplift, or emotion.

2. *Gestures below the shoulders* indicate sadness, rejection, apathy, or condemnation.

3. *Gestures at or near the shoulders* suggest a calmness or serenity.

The most frequently used gestures involve an open palm held outward toward the audience. Holding your palm outward implies giving or receiving something. Unfortunately, this sort of gesture is used unconsciously by many speakers as movement without any specific meaning.

A palm held *downward* expresses suppression, secrecy, completion, stability, or a covering over.

A palm held *upward* and *outward* suggests halting or repulsion. The hands can also be used to imply measurement (e.g., tall, small, long).

Don't Keep Your Hands to Yourself

There are speakers who, with a well-placed gesture, can move an audience to the edge of their seats. For many speakers, however, the only body movements included in presentations are the frantic clutching of note cards and the grasping of the lectern for support.

Body movements can make or break a presentation. You can motivate your audience through well-timed gestures, pacing, and, of course, eye contact. The problem is that most presenters keep their gestures very close to their bodies and do not use large enough gestures. They may raise their hands but do so in a limp manner and without any enthusiasm. All presenters, especially those with little experience, keep their movements restricted and within a tight comfort zone. In Figure 6.1 I have defined our natural comfort zone.

When we first present, we tend to restrict the degree to which we gesture within a very small comfort zone. The more anxious a presenter a person is, the smaller and tighter the comfort zone. This comfort zone varies from presenter to presenter, but in most cases, the natural comfort zone is too small for your gestures to be effective and easily seen by the audience.

The challenge is to force yourself to step out of your comfort zone and use bigger gestures. As a novice or inexperienced presenter, this is more difficult to do because we want to stay in our natural comfort zone. When we do use more energy and go

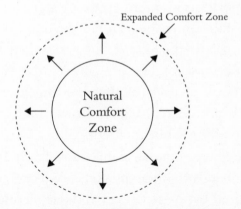

Figure 6.1 Comfort zone. To be more dynamic, presenters need to use larger gestures outside their comfort zone. In other words, exaggerate what you want to do naturally.

outside our natural comfort zone, we think we are gesturing too much, when, in fact, we are not. Most speakers believe that they use gestures too much when they are not using them enough.

To use more effective gestures, all you need to do is to gesture exactly the way you naturally do but make the gestures bigger. For example, if you take a 6-inch step forward to emphasize a point, next time take a 12-inch step instead—same motion, same direction, but bigger. Gestures should consist of purposeful movements of the head, shoulders, arms, hands, and entire body.

What Do I Do with My Hands When I Am Not Gesturing?

Many presenters say, "I never know what to do with my hands when I am not talking." Most people are not sure where to put their hands and feel very uncomfortable. It is very important to find a good resting position. There is no right resting position, and you may like to use more than one type of resting position.

The resting position is where you start and end your gesture. Most gestures start from the center of your body and move out, up, down, or to the side. I have provided you with the top six resting position used by presenters today (see Figures 6.2 through 6.7). Look at each of these resting positions. Notice that your hands are centered in front of your body, at waist level. Your arms should also be bent.

All too often, when men stand up to speak, the first thing they do is put their hands in their pockets. As they continue their presentations, their hands go deeper and deeper and deeper until then cannot go any farther. When they eventually try to use their hands to gesture, they find that their hands are buried so deep in their pockets that they have difficulty getting them out.

Figure 6.2   Nondescript or open resting position. Hands held at waist level with palms up.

As discussed earlier, there is also the habit of playing with pocket change. The only person this appeases is the person playing with the change in the pocket. Many women have a habit of playing with their jewelry, hair, or clothes. They are either tugging with an earring, brushing their hair back with their fingers, or pulling their suit jacket down. Each of these habits can be distracting to an audience. Practice using each of the resting positions shown and see which ones are most comfortable to you. Try not to use only one type of resting position. Use a couple because this will give your audience a different look.

Figure 6.3 The prayer position. Hands held at waist level and folded.

HOW TO GESTURE EFFECTIVELY

Gestures are reflections of every speaker's individual personality. What's right for one presenter, may not feel right for another; however, the following six rules apply to anyone who seeks to become a dynamic presenter:

Rule 1: Respond naturally to what you think, feel, and see. It is natural for you to gesture, and it's unnatural for you to not gesture. Each if us gestures every day whether or not we are thinking about it. Using gestures should come

Figure 6.4   The spider or steeple position. Hands held at waist level with fingertips lightly touching.

natural. When you inhibit your movement and hold back your desire to gesture, you'll probably become tense. Let the gesture happen naturally but try to exaggerate the gesture slightly to give it more dynamics.

Rule 2: Create the condition for gesturing, not the gesture itself. When you speak, you should be totally involved with communicating and not thinking about your hands. Your gestures should be motivated by the content of your presentation.

Rule 3: Suit the action to the word and the occasion. Your visual and verbal messages must function as partners in communicating the same thought or feeling. Every gesture

Figure 6.5   The opera singer position. Hands held at waist level with hands clasped.

you make should be purposeful and reflective of your words so that the audience will note only the effect, not the gesture itself. Do not overdo your gestures, or you will draw the listener away from your message. Younger audiences are usually attracted to a presenter who uses vigorous gestures. Older, more conservative groups may feel irritated or threatened by a presenter whose physical actions are overwhelming.

Rule 4: Make your gestures convincing. Your gestures should be lively and distinct if they are to convey the intended impressions. Effective gestures are vigorous enough to be convincing yet slow enough and broad enough to be clearly visible without being overpowering.

**Figure 6.6   The fig leaf position. Hands crossed just
below waist level.**

Rule 5: Make your gestures smooth and well timed. Every
gesture has three parts:

- *The approach:* Your body begins to move in anticipation.
- *The stroke:* The gesture itself.
- *The return:* This brings your body back to a balanced
resting position.

    The flow of a gesture—the approach, the stroke,
the return—must be smoothly executed so that only the
stroke is evident to the audience. Although it is advisable
to practice gesturing, don't try to memorize your every

Figure 6.7   The reversed fig leaf position. Hands crossed behind back at waist level.

move. This makes your gesturing stilted and ineffective. The last rule is probably the most important but also the hardest.

Rule 6: Make natural, spontaneous gesturing a habit. The first step in becoming adept at gesturing is to determine what, if anything, you are doing now. The best way to discover this is to record yourself presenting. Recording yourself can help you identify any of your bad habits. Make a list of the mannerisms you want to eliminate and work at eliminating them one at a time. You will need to continue recording yourself and

146

evaluate your progress if you expect to eliminate all your distracting mannerisms. To improve your gestures, you need to practice, but not during an actual presentation. Practice presenting informally to friends, family, members, and coworkers.

BODY MOVEMENT

Changing your position or location while speaking is the broadest, most visible kind of physical action you, as a presenter, can perform. Because of this, it can be either a tremendous asset or a tremendous liability to your delivery.

When you speak, you can benefit three ways by moving your entire body in a controlled, purposeful manner.

- Body movement can support and reinforce what you say.
- Body movement always attracts an audience attention.
- Body movement is the fastest, most effective means of burning up nervous energy and relieving physical tension.

Body movement can also work against you. If there is one rule about this, it is:

Never move without a reason.

The eye is inevitably attracted to a moving object, so any body movement you make during a speech invites attention. Too much movement, even the right kind, can become distracting to an audience.

- *Stepping forward* during a presentation suggests you are arriving at an important point.
- *Stepping backward* indicates you've concluded an idea and are willing to allow the audience to relax for a moment.

- *Lateral movement* implies a transition; it indicates that you are leaving one thought and taking up another.

The final reason for body movement is perhaps the simplest: *to get from one place to another.* In almost every presentation, you must walk to and from the point where you deliver your presentation (especially if you use visual aids). Always change positions by leading with the foot nearest to your destination.

Five Ways to Make Your Body Speak Effectively

Rid Yourself of Distracting Mannerisms

Dr. Ralph C. Smeadly, the founder of Toastmasters International, wrote, "The speaker who stands and talks at ease is the one who can be heard without weariness. If his posture and gestures are so graceful and unobtrusive, that no one notices them, he may be counted as truly successful."

When your actions are wedded to your words, the impact of your presentation will be strengthened. If your platform behavior includes mannerisms unrelated to your spoken message, those actions will call attention to themselves and away from your presentation. Eliminate vocal and visual impediments.

Some common faults of inexperienced or ineffective speakers are:

- Gripping or leaning on the lectern
- Tapping fingers
- Biting or licking lips
- Playing with coins or jewelry
- Frowning
- Adjusting hair or clothing
- Head wagging

These all have two things in common:

- They are physical manifestations of simple nervousness.
- They are performed unconsciously.

Recording Yourself

The best and most effective way to improve your presenting is to record your presentation and review it, paying attention to your body language, movement, gestures, tone of voice, and overall performance. Here is a list of specific elements you should look for when reviewing your recording:

1. Posture
2. Gestures
3. Body movement
4. Facial expressions
5. Eye contact
6. Voice

Remember, the first step in eliminating any superfluous mannerisms or language is to get an accurate perception of your body language and voice. Sit with a notepad and write down everything you notice on the video about your body language and voice.

Review 1: Review the recording without looking for particular mannerisms. Just listen to the presentation as if you were hearing it for the first time, and evaluate the *overall impact* you experience from watching the video. During this initial review, pretend you are a member of the audience and evaluate your reaction to the presentation, trying to separate the fact that you are watching yourself. This will be difficult. Here are a few questions to think about and ask yourself during this review.

- Did I like the presentation?
- Was it informative or entertaining?
- Would I recommend someone else watch the video?

Review 2: Turn off the sound and look only for *visual distractions.* Jot down notes about what you observe. Make two lists, one for the things you liked and another for the things you did not like. Don't worry if your list of cons is longer; each time you give a presentation your performance will improve. Look specifically for the following:

- What did you do with your hands?
- What were your facial expressions?
- What did you do with your body?
- Did you move around? Did you stand still?
- Were there any mannerisms you found distracting or annoying?
- Did you seem appropriately animated?

Review 3: Darken the picture or turn your back to the screen so that you cannot see yourself and listen only to your voice. Many people have never heard their own voice on a recording. Become accustomed to the sound of your voice. Your first reaction may be, "That does not sound like me!" When you hear your voice for the first time, you are hearing it from "inside" your head. While listening to your voice, focus on the following:

- What do you like and not like about your voice?

- How was the speed of your speaking? Was it too fast or too slow?

- How was your tone of voice?

- How was your pitch? Was it too high or too low?

Review 4: After you have completed your list of pros and cons, ask one or two family members to watch the video with you. Get their initial impression. Have them take their own notes, and when the video is finished, compare notes. Keep this list handy and tackle each negative point one at a time. Also remember to make a note of the positive comments!

Another important step is to gather all the notes and make another list. This is a list of those areas you believe need improvement. Make sure you are as specific as possible. Now take the items on the list and break them down into the following categories:

- *Voice and tone:* This includes the tone of your voice, speed, pitch, and any verbal distractions such as uhms, uhs, ers, and ya knows.

- *Nonverbal actions:* Break these down by body parts, such as your hands, facial expressions, legs, arms, walking patterns, and so on, and list them specifically. Don't be surprised if the list is long. That's okay. All speakers will have a long list when they first begin giving presentations. With practice, practice, and more practice, you eventually will see fewer areas in need of improvement. Look at the list and prioritize what areas you want to start working on immediately.

Make a conscious note of these areas and observe and listen to how you speak during your everyday activities. The next time you are at a party, at a business meeting, or with a friend, see if you notice any of these distracting mannerisms. Also, do you notice any of these distractions while talking on the phone?

Each time you speak, make an effort to eliminate or replace the distracting mannerism with a verbal or nonverbal technique. Practice every day. By making adjustments and changes in your everyday speaking style, you will find it easier to apply these strategies to your more formal speaking engagements, such as presentations at work, a toast at a wedding, or a speech to a large group.

Another helpful tip is to keep a journal after each presentation. Take a few moments to reflect on your presentation. Make notes about your strengths and weaknesses and write a brief summary on your speech topic, the audience, and any other factors that will come in handy for future presentations.

Build Self-Confidence by Being Yourself

The most important rule for making your body communicate effectively is to be yourself by being conversational. The emphasis should be on the sharing of ideas and not on the performance. Strive to be as genuine and natural as you are when you speak to family members and friends.

Large versus Small Audiences

Many people say, "I'm okay in a small group, but when I get in front of a larger group I freeze." Other people do not like small intimate groups. Each person is different. The only difference between speaking to a small informal group and to a sizable audience is the number of listeners. To compensate for this, you need only to amplify your natural behavior by increasing your comfort zone.

Be authentically yourself, but amplify your movements and expressions just enough that the audience can see them.

Let Your Body Mirror Your Feelings

If you are interested in your subject, truly believe what you are saying, and want to share your message with others, your physical movements will come from within you and will be appropriate to what you are saying.

By involving yourself in your message, you'll be natural and spontaneous without having to consciously think about what you are doing or saying. For many of us, this isn't as easy as it sounds because it requires us to drop the mask that shields the "real self" in public.

To become an effective presenter, it is essential that you get rid of your mask and share your true feelings with your audience. Your audience wants to know how *you* feel about your subject. If you want to convince others, you must convey *your* convictions.

Speak from the heart and speak to the soul.

Build Self-Confidence through Preparation

Nothing influences a speaker's mental attitude more than the knowledge that he or she is thoroughly prepared. This knowledge leads to self-confidence, which is a vital ingredient of effective public speaking.

Have you ever experienced a situation in which you had not prepared well for a presentation? How did it come across?

Contrast those presentations with those that *did* go well. Those are the ones that you had prepared for.

Use Your Everyday Speaking Situations to Help You

Whenever you speak to people, make an extra effort to notice *how* you speak. Observe, too, whether the facial expressions of your listeners indicate they do or do not understand what you are saying. Before calling to request something on the phone, plan and practice what you are going to say. Even this is essentially a short presentation.

Another exercise is to prepare a 90-second presentation about yourself. Describe who you are and what you do. Record your presentation and review it using the four steps described earlier. Since you are talking about yourself, you do not need to research the topic; however, you do need to prepare what you are going to say and how you are going to say it. Plan everything, including your gestures and walking patterns.

Facial Expressions

Leave the deadpan expression to poker players. A speaker realizes that appropriate facial expressions are an important part of effective communication. In fact, facial expressions are often the key determinant of the meaning behind the message. People watch a presenter's face during a presentation. When you speak, your face, more clearly than other parts of your body, communicates to others your attitudes, feelings, and emotions.

Remove expressions that don't belong to your face.

Inappropriate facial expressions include distracting mannerisms or unconscious expressions not rooted in your feelings, attitudes, and emotions. In much the same way that some speakers perform random, distracting gestures and body movements, nervous speakers often release excess energy and tension by unconsciously moving their facial muscles (e.g., licking lips, tightening of the jaw).

One type of unconscious facial movement that is less apt to be read clearly by an audience is involuntary frowning. This type of frowning occurs when a presenter attempts to deliver a memorized speech.

There are no rules governing the use of specific expressions. If you relax your inhibitions and allow yourself to respond naturally to your thoughts, attitudes, and emotions, your facial expressions will be appropriate and will project sincerity, conviction, and credibility.

In 1976, Dr. Paul Eckman, along with Wallace Friesen, developed what is called the Facial Action Coding System (FACS). Dr. Eckman's work has shown that the face can communicate more than 40,000 expressions. This FACS system is the most popular standard currently used to systematically categorize the physical expression of emotions, and it has proved useful to both psychologists and to many other professionals. Those who may be interested in Dr. Eckman's work will find his research to be very fascinating.

Eye Contact

Eye contact is the cement that binds together presenters and their audiences. When you speak, your eyes involve your listeners in your presentation. There is no surer way to break a communication bond between you and the audience than by failing to look at your listeners. No matter how large your audience may be, each listener wants to feel that you are talking to him or her.

The adage "The eyes are the mirror to the soul" underlines the need for you to convince people with your eyes, as well as with your words. Only by looking at your listeners as individuals can you convince them that you are sincere, are interested in them, and care whether they accept your message.

When you speak, your eyes also function as a control device you can use to ensure your listeners' attentiveness and concentration. Eye contact can also help you overcome nervousness by making your audience a known quantity. Effective eye contact is an important feedback device that makes the speaking situation a two-way communication process. By looking at your audience, you can determine how they are reacting. When you develop the ability to gauge the audience's reactions and adjust your presentation accordingly, you will be a much more effective presenter.

How to Use Your Eyes Effectively

1. *Know your material.* Know your material so well that you don't have to devote your mental energy to the task of remembering the sequence of ideas and words. You should prepare well (remember the nine Ps in Chapter 3) and rehearse enough that you don't have to depend heavily on notes. Many speakers, no matter how well prepared, need at least a few notes to deliver their message. If you can speak effectively without notes, by all means do so. If you must use notes, that's fine. Just do not let them be a substitute for preparation and rehearsal. When experienced presenters use notes, they often take advantage of natural pauses such as audience laughter or the aftermath of an important point to glance briefly at their notes. To make this technique work, keep your notes brief.

2. *Establish a personal bond with listeners.* How do you do this? Begin by selecting one person and talking to him or her personally. Maintain eye contact with that person long enough to establish a visual bond (about three to five seconds). This is usually the equivalent of a sentence or a thought. Then shift your gaze to another person. In a small group, this is relatively easy to do. But, if you're addressing hundreds or thousands of people, it's impossible. What you can do is pick out one or two individuals in each section of the room and establish personal bonds with them. Then each listener will get the impression you're talking directly to him or her.

3. *Monitor visual feedback.* While you are talking, your listeners are responding with their own nonverbal messages. Use your eyes to actively seek out this valuable feedback. If individuals aren't looking at you, they may not be listening either. Their reasons may include one or more of these factors:

They may not be able to hear you.

Solution: If you are not using a microphone, speak louder and note if that works.

■ ■ ■

They may be bored.

Solution: Use some humor, increase your vocal variety or add powerful gestures or body movements.

■ ■ ■

They may be puzzled.

Solution: Repeat and/or rephrase what you have just said.

■ ■ ■

They seem to be fidgeting nervously.

Solution: You may be using distracting mannerisms. Maybe you have food on your clothes (or worse, maybe your blouse in unbuttoned or your fly isn't closed). Make sure you are aware of these embarrassing possibilities before and during your presentation. If necessary, try to correct them without bringing more attention to them. On the other hand, if your listeners' faces indicate pleasure, interest, and close attention, don't change a thing. You're doing a great job!

Your Appearance

If your listeners will be wearing suits and dresses, wear your best suit or dress—the outfit that brings you the most compliments. Make sure that every item of clothing is clean and well-tailored. Don't wear jewelry that might glitter or jingle when you move or gesture. This might divert attention away from your presentation. For the same reason, empty your pockets of bulky items and anything that will make noise when you move.

Part of the first impression you give occurs even before you are introduced to deliver your presentation. As the audience arrives, your preparation should be concluded. You should not have to study your presentation. Instead, mingle with the audience, and project that same friendly, confident attitude that will make your presentation a success.

When you present, especially if you aren't well known to the audience, the most crucial part of your presentation is the first few minutes. During that initial segment, the audience will be making critical judgments about you. Your listeners will decide whether you are confident, sincere, friendly, eager to address them, and worthy of their attention. In large measure, they will base this decision on what they see. After your introduction, walk purposely and confidently to the speaking position.

Walking Patterns

Why move in the first place? Moving forces people to focus and follow you. The way you walk from your seat to the speaker's position is very important. When you are introduced, you should appear eager to speak. Too many speakers look as though they are heading toward their execution.

Walk confidently from your seat to the lectern. Pause there for a few seconds, then move out from behind the lectern. As discussed before, it is wise to use the lectern as a point of departure, not as a barrier to hide behind. Smile before you say your first words. Be careful not to stand too close to, or move beyond, the people in the front row.

Be careful not to walk too much. Continuous pacing is very distracting and will work against you. Purposeful walking, on the other hand, can be an effective way to stress an important idea. It is essential that your walk have intent and not just be a random shift of position. Taking about three steps, moving at a shallow angle, usually works best.

When using visual aids, use three positions. One position is your "home" position and should be front and center. The other two positions should be relatively near the home position. Never stand in front of any visual aid. When you are practicing your presentation, make sure you also practice your walking patterns. Try walking to and from your three positions. These positions should be planned just as your hand gestures are. When standing still, remember to maintain good posture. Stand up straight.

CHAPTER 7

How to Handle Questions

QUESTION-AND-ANSWER PERIOD

When developing your presentation, it is critical to prepare for the possible questions your audience may ask you during and after the presentation. This includes not only expected and regular questions but also questions that may be difficult to answer.

In the next few pages, I will provide you with a structure and format for both types of questions: regular, or straightforward, questions, and difficult, or hostile, questions.

THE FIVE-STEP PROCESS FOR ANSWERING REGULAR (NONDIFFICULT) QUESTIONS

Many presenters like to avoid the question-and-answer period following a presentation. For some presenters, this is the most dreaded part of the presentation. For others, this can be the most exciting part of the presentation. If you did a good job with your presentation, you will see your audience eagerly wanting to ask questions.

When dealing with questions, I like to use this five-step process:

Step 1: Listen to the entire question. When someone asks you a question, listen to the entire question carefully. If you could not hear the question, ask the person to repeat it. While you listen, listen to the tone of the person's voice. Is it calm, is it reasonably normal, or is it angry or upset? Do not only listen to the words, but also watch the person's demeanor while he or she asks the question. Notice the person's body language.

Step 2: Repeat the entire question. Regardless of how large or small the audience is, repeat the entire question. You should repeat the question for three reasons:

1. By repeating the question, it allows everyone in your audience to be able to hear the entire question. How many times have you ever sat in the audience during a presentation and someone in the front row asks a question that you cannot hear? This happens all the time. Repeating the question allows the entire audience to hear the question.

2. By repeating the question, you gain additional time to think about and evaluate the question.

3. By repeating the question, you have more time to decide how you will answer and determine exactly what you want to say.

Step 3: Pause for a moment. Collect your thoughts, smile, and take a deep breath. This should not be a long pause but a short pause. Do not immediately start answering the question. Many presenters have a tendency to quickly start responding without taking a pause. Presenters tend to begin responding quickly to those questions they know the answer to and are very comfortable with. It is the difficult questions or the hostile questions we are asked that we respond very slowly to. You should get into the practice of pausing for the same amount of time after each question, regardless of whether it is a regular question or a difficult one. When you do this, you avoid bringing attention to those questions you stumble with and find more difficult.

Step 4: Answer or respond to the question. Respond to the question as professionally as you can, maintaining eye contact with the audience member who asked you the question. While you answer the question, also establish eye contact with the rest of the audience. If you do not know the answer to the question, be honest and say, "Sorry but I do not know the answer to your questions; however, let me get back to you. Is that okay with you?" At this point you can write down the person's name or ask that person to come see you after the presentation to get his or her contact information.

Step 5: After you have responded to a question, you should bridge to the next question. You create this bridge by asking the person if you answered the question. You can say this in many different ways. "Does that help you?" "Is that the type of answer you were looking for?" and so on. Once the person says "yes" or nods in agreement, this gives you permission to move on to the next question. If the person says "no," ask him or her to rephrase the question. Repeat the process as described earlier until the person is satisfied with your response.

What If No One Asks You Any Questions?

After you have completed your presentation and are transitioning to the question–and–answer period, there may be times when you ask the audience if they have any questions and wait and wait and wait but no one raises a hand. You might have a tendency to say yourself, "Thank God," and make a quick exit. In my experience and in most situations, you will find that no one in your audience wants to be the first person to ask you a question. In these cases, I actually throw out the first question. It may start out something like this, "Many people have asked me . . ." I then respond to that question as if someone from the audience actually asked me that question. I would offer one word of caution when you do use this technique: make sure you ask a question you can actually answer. You laugh but I have seen this happen to a few presenters. It is pretty embarrassing to be unable to answer your own question.

Another option is to avoid this uncomfortable situation all together—the silence can be deafening when no one immediately volunteers a question—or at least lessen the void by taking the following measures:

1. Hand out question cards at the beginning of your presentation.

2. Take an information survey ("How many of you . . . ?")

3. Pose your question ("A question I am frequently asked is . . .")

4. To arouse curiosity, deliberately omit an obvious part of your presentation.

5. Arrange with the program chairperson to select an audience member ahead of time to ask the first question.

6. If you have paused for questions before concluding your presentation, you can simply end by saying, "If there are no questions, let me share one final thought with you."

DEALING WITH DIFFICULT OR HOSTILE QUESTIONS

There will be times when the questions you are asked are difficult or even hostile. How you handle these types of questions is a little different. Keep in mind, that in many cases, the questions your audience will want to ask you may be difficult and it is your responsibility to provide answers to these questions. How you personally handle these questions can either add to or detract from your credibility as a speaker.

There are a few techniques that are typically used when dealing with difficult questions. I will first describe each technique and then provide you with an example.

Technique 1: The Delay Tactic

Say someone asks you a question that you do not want to answer immediately. This may be because (1) you do not know the answer to the question or (2) you do not want to answer the question because you need time to think about the answer. What some speakers do, and this a technique I see politicians use all the time, is to immediately turn their attention to someone else who had just asked a question and say something like this (while looking at the person who asked them a question earlier), "You asked me a question earlier about . . ." At this point, when you are the speaker, you can respond by providing additional information to the question you were asked earlier. What you are actually doing is stalling for time as you think about how you will answer the difficult question. This is an attempt to buy some time to formulate your answer or response to the difficult question. You then go back and ask the person who asked you the difficult question to repeat the question again (again you are stalling for additional time). You are now better prepared to respond to this question. One word of caution; you can probably use this technique only once during your question-and-answer period. This also assumes that you were listening carefully to the question earlier and still are thinking about the response to that question in the back of your mind.

Technique 2: The Compound Question Tactic

There will be times when someone in your audience says to you, "I have a two questions. The first question is [question 1] and the second part of the question is [question 2]." This is not uncommon with presentations, and I have experienced this type of question many times. When I talk about this type of question during my presentation skills classes, I ask the participants in my class, and I will ask you the same now: Which question should I answer first? The first question or the second? (Here is where I am giving you a few seconds to think.)

My response to this question is, I always answer the easier question first. Keep in mind that the easier of the two questions may not always be the first question. I respond to the easier question, and then I ask them to repeat the other question (this is where I am using technique 1 to stall a little).

So what if you do not know the answer to one of the questions? What you *do not* do is say something like this, "Well I do not know the answer to the first question, so let me deal with the second part of your question." Under no circumstance should you do this. What you are better off doing is to say something like this, "Let me deal with the second part of your question first." You then respond to the second part of the question. Once you answered the second part of the question, you then ask them to repeat the first question. You then can respond to this question and if, for some reason, you do not know the answer to this part of the question, it won't appear as awkward.

Technique 3: The Diffusion Tactic

When you are faced with a difficult question that borders on being hostile, you use a diffusion technique. Say you are discussing a point of view and someone asks you a hostile question.

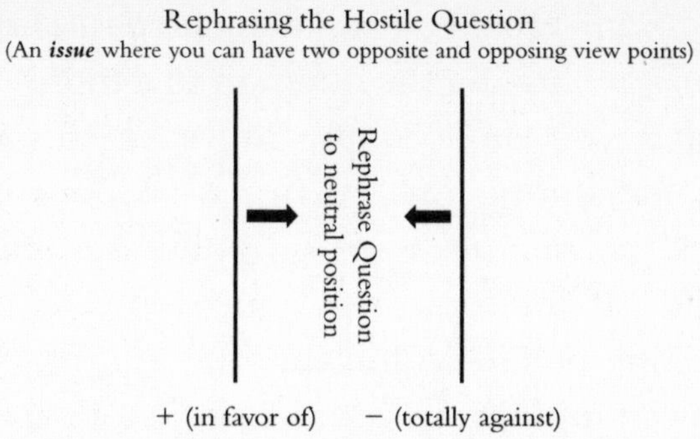

Rephrasing the Hostile Question
(An *issue* where you can have two opposite and opposing view points)

+ (in favor of)   − (totally against)

Figure 7.1   You want to rephrase the hostile question to a more neutral position (regardless of your personal position) and then respond to the rephrased question.

(I will provide you with an example in a little while.) What you want to do is to (1) listen to the entire question, (2) think carefully about the question, and then (3) rephrase the question to a more neutral position. Referring to Figure 7.1, let me give you an actual example of a difficult question.

Many times the difficult question may arise from a very strong opposing viewpoint. Say, for example, you are in favor of an issue, and the audience member is clearly not in favor of the issue. You are on opposite sides. Your goal is to first understand where the other person is coming from and where his or her reference point is. You do this by first seeking to understand where the person is coming from without verbally passing any judgment. After asking a few clarifying questions, you will get a better idea and then can respond; however, in many cases, you do not want to engage in a dialog to do this, so you need to carefully listen to the question, make a quick mental assessment, and carefully rephrase the question to a more neutral tone without really changing the meaning of the question. After carefully rephrasing the question, you then respond to your rephrased question. What you are doing here is (1) repeating the question but (2) rephrasing the question to a more neutral tone.

Let me give you an example to make this clearer. Say someoneasks me during one of my workshops or seminars, "What makes *you such an expert* on public speaking and presentation skills?" If you look at this question carefully, you will note that the one phrase within this question is, "you such an expert." You can just hear in your head the tone in the person's voice while asking this question. What I do not want to do is to repeat this question exactly how it was asked. This would not diffuse or neutralize anything. After listening to this question carefully, I would repeat the question but rephrase it as, "You are probably wondering where I got all my speaking experience." Look at my rephrased question closely. I replaced the "you such an expert" with "where I got all my speaking experience." I would then respond to my rephrased question. Notice how I shifted the focus from me being an expert to one who has a lot of speaking experience.

Applying this technique smoothly and professionally will take some practice. Although this is not as hostile of a question as some can be, it does give you an example of how to apply the technique. During my workshops, I have each of the participants get up and try this technique while responding to questions from the other participants.

Technique 4: Just Agree with Them

One very powerful technique you can use when someone asks a difficult question or even makes a difficult statement is to just outright agree with the person (assuming you do agree). Many times, someone is not really asking you a question but making a statement, such as, "I really feel that [whatever the issue is] is stupid." Your response (again only if you agree) is, "You're right! It is stupid." Then pause. This allows the other person to realize you just agreed, which will probably be a shock. You then soon follow up you response with, "However, I have found . . ." You then provide some sage advice or response at this point. The key here is to show you agree first, but then you offer a solution for dealing with the issue. This technique can take the wind right out of the person's sail.

How Do I Diffuse Hostility?

1. *Make sure you have been understood.* Restate your position so that it is clear in the minds of the audience.

2. *Be poised and positive.* Shift the focus from the points of conflict toward the more fundamental principles on which we can all agree. Help the audience to attain agreement with you on principles and indisputable facts, and they will agree with you more readily on following points of the presentation.

3. *Eliminate conflicting ideas by illustrating the commonality of the audience's goals and your goals.* Clarify the problem or argument from the audience's point of view. Try to change their view of the situation from a black-and-white one to a viewpoint that allows for some shades of gray. Be sure to do this in a helpful, informative manner. Never become argumentative.

4. *Ally yourself with positive symbols.* Controversial issues always involve symbols, and the side most effectively associated with positive symbols—such as law, economic security, and conversation—will be more likely to prevail. Try to relate your side to emotional symbols as a powerful aid to your persuasive appeal.

5. *Tactfully refute the opposition.* You need to counter the opposition's arguments that already have convinced your audience. This should be done in a nonthreatening manner. Avoid any statement that could be interpreted as a personal attack on your audience or their association. Illustrate ways in which adopting your point of view will be more helpful to them personally than if they choose to follow the opposition. In other words, appeal to their self-interest.

More Tips on Handling Hostile Questions

1. *Be truthful.* If you try to bend the truth, you will almost always be caught. Play it straight, even if your position seems momentarily weakened.

2. *Be friendly.* Always control your temper. A cool presentation creates an aura of confidence. When the questioner is hostile, respond as though he or she were a friend. Any attempt to "put down" your questioner with sarcasm will immediately draw the audience's sympathy to the questioner.

3. *Be fair.* Take questions from all parts of an audience. Don't limit yourself to front rows and don't let one person monopolize the available time.

4. *Don't place your hands on your hips and don't point at the audience.* Both of these are scolding poses and have the appearance of preaching.

5. *Avoid condescending phrases.*

6. *Quit while you're ahead.* Don't exceed the allotted time. Keep an eye on the clock or have someone signal you. Be prepared to give appropriate closing remarks.

CHAPTER 8

The Effective Speech

It has been observed that half the world is composed of people who have something to say and can't, while the other half have nothing to say and keep saying it. Anyone can give a speech, but certainly not everyone can give an *effective* presentation. As mentioned earlier, public speaking is not a gift you are born with. Fortunately, giving effective presentations is a skill you can acquire.

Following are some tips for developing and delivering an effective speech:

1. Find your objective. Your objective or message must be clear to you and your audience.

2. Know you audience. Take the time to determine who will be in your audience and what they want to know and learn.

3. Be totally prepared. You owe it to your audience to provide them with the best presentation.

4. Hook your audience instantly. Take the time to create an effective opening.

5. Plan your gestures and body movements. Once you have developed your content, work on the gestures that will effectively work with your content.

6. Use good delivery techniques.

7. Cite personal examples whenever possible. Use personal stories to support your messages and key points.

8. Maintain a sharp focus.

9. Speak persuasively.

10. Keep a positive attitude.

11. Add impact with visuals.

12. Follow up for success.

MORE ON PREPARATION AND PRESENTATION

Being totally prepared includes eliminating surprises that can lead to nervousness and forgetfulness. It means knowing your destination, your audience, and your material.

To avoid last-minute jitters:

- Always arrive at least one hour early.

- Make sure you have the right location (school, hotel, or room).

- Arrive early enough that you have time to check out the speaking environment. Doing this early will allow you to make adjustments if needed.

- If you need audiovisual equipment, it is your responsibility to tell the meeting planner.

- Provide instructions in advance regarding how you would like the room arranged.

- Be prepared to use more than one type of visual aid.

- Check out all your equipment.

- Learn how to control the lights in the room.

Remembering and Relating the Presentation Material

There are four common ways to remember the content of your presentation:

- Memorizing

- Reading from complete text

- Referring to notes
- Using visual aids as notes

Memorizing

Memorizing is absolutely the worst way to keep track of your presentation material. You can become so preoccupied with the words you are saying that you lose the actual ideas behind the words. When you memorize material, you will find yourself thinking more about remembering your material than relating to your audience. Normal voice inflection disappears in the process, and worse, those terrible blank moments are inevitable. It's not a matter of "Am I going to forget?" but, "When am I going to forget?"

Reading from Complete Text

Most people hate listening to someone read a presentation. The reason is simple: "If all they are going to do is read the slides to me, I could have read the slides myself." On top of that, many presenters read poorly. Why do you think speakers fair so poorly when reading? For a variety of reasons:

- *The speaker loses normal voice inflection.* Speakers who read often lose touch with the ideas behind the words. Listen for pauses. Natural speaking is filled with pauses; stilted reading is not.

- *The text isn't spoken language.* Too often speakers write their presentations in "business-ease," that gobbledygook that is hard to read, much less listen to.

- *The speech is static.* The potted plant will probably move more. There is little energy behind the lectern.

- *There is no eye contact.* Any eye contact is with the text and not the audience.

- *The speaker is scared.* Some speakers read because they are afraid to try anything else. They know reading will fail, but at least it will fail with a small "f" rather than a capital one.

Of course, there are some occasions when a speaker *must* read. This applies when one must communicate precise policy or company statements. There are also times when a speech has to be timed down to the second, and a script is therefore used. When you must read, try to sound natural. Rehearse often, check for pauses, and ask yourself whether the words you are using are typical of everyday conversation rather than "business-ease." Plan for gestures. For example, you could point in the general direction of the city you are mentioning, indicate how small something is, shrug at the right time, or raise an eyebrow when appropriate.

You may choose to put cues for these gestures into the text. If your text is user-friendly, you will have a better chance of making eye contact with your audience. Make the paragraphs short so that you don't lose your place every time you look up. Avoid using capital letters because these are harder to read. Use a larger type size. Do not staple pages together. Rather, use a paperclip because this allows you to slide the pages from side to side.

Referring to Notes

The most common technique for remembering material is to use notes. Using notes is better than reading because the speaker can have normal voice inflection and make eye contact more easily. Sometimes, if the notes are on the lectern, speakers won't move very far from it. On the other hand, if speakers hold their notes in their hands, they probably won't gesture very much.

If you chose to use note cards, include quotes, statistics, and lists on them. Do not put too much information on each note card. Leave your notes on the lectern or table and move away from them occasionally. If you find yourself reading the note cards too much, you probably have too much information on them. Revise them to contain only short phrases or words. Some speakers even use pictures, picture maps, or mind maps to jog their memories.

Using Visual Aids as Notes

Simple visual aids serve as headings and subheadings. Speak to the heading, say what you want to say and then move on. If you forget something, that's all right. The audience will not know you've slipped.

Using visual aids has important advantages:

1. *You don't have to worry about what you are going to say next.* This is perhaps the most significant advantage. You can concentrate on the point at hand, knowing your visual summarizes your next major idea.

2. *You can move around the room.* Inexperienced speakers do not want to move around, but movement helps you relax and adds energy to your presentations. Movement also allows the audience to follow you and to pay closer attention to you.

3. *You can have good eye contact with your audience.* You can look at your audience all the time, except when you are looking briefly at your visual aid. Of course, the audience too will be focusing on the visual aid at that time. There is always an advantage to having the audience both see and hear the message.

4. *Your audience feels comfortable knowing you are on a planned track.* Well-designed visual aids show you have properly prepared a plan and are following it.

Transitions

Transitions are an integral part of a smooth-flowing presentation, yet many speakers forget to plan their transitions. The primary purpose of a transition is to lead your listener from one idea to another. The following are some examples of transitions that work well:

1. *Bridge words:* Examples include *furthermore, meanwhile, however, in addition, consequently*, and *finally*.

2. *Trigger transition:* Use the same word or idea twice. For example, "a similar example is . . ."

3. *A question:* "How many of you . . . ?"

4. *A flashback:* "Do you remember when I said . . . ?"

5. *Point-by-point:* "There are three points . . . The first one is . . . The second one is . . . ," and so on.

6. *Visual aids:* Sometimes it may be appropriate to add a visual between your visual aids for the sole purpose of providing a "visual" transition. Many times just a blank screen, as is used when using slides, works well.

7. *Pausing:* Even a simple pause, when effectively used, can act as a transition.

8. *Physical movement:* The speaker should move or change location of his or her body when changing to a new idea or thought.

9. *A story:* The use of a story is very effective as a transition. It is also used to reinforce any points you just made.

10. *PEP formula (point, example, point):* This is a very common format used and also can be combined with the use of a story.

Three Common Mistakes Made When Using Transitions

Transitions are short descriptions that presenters use to segue from one section of a presentation to another. Many presenters simply advance to the next slide without providing any lead-in or setup of the next slide. Transitions, when used effectively, act like the glue that smoothly binds each of the visual aids together.

Following are the top three common mistakes presenters make with respect to transitions:

1. They do not use transitions at all. Transitions help your information flow from one idea to the next.

2. They use transitions that are too short. Not enough time is spent in bridging from one idea to the next. This is extremely important when changing to a new section of ideas within your presentation.

3. They use the same transition throughout the presentation. This becomes boring after a while. Try being creative with your transitions.

Transitions and the Team Presentation

Transitions become extremely important when a team presentation is involved. The transition from one speaker to the next must be planned and executed skillfully. Each speaker should provide a brief introduction of the next topic and speaker as part of this transition. Having smooth transitions from one team member to the next further adds to the smoothness of the presentation. These transitions should also be rehearsed and practiced along with the presentation itself.

The Use of Humor

Another element of successful presentations is the inclusion of humor. When I talk about humor, I am not talking about using jokes. The inclusion of humorous quotes, stories, or even expressions can add a lot to a presentation. Few people remember a dry presentation, so use humor when at all possible. It does not need to be used a lot but used sparingly.

Not all of us are comedians, nor should we try to be. If using humor is not something you are comfortable with, then do not use it. Never tell dirty or off-color jokes. These will always offend someone and should be avoided all together.

Two ideal locations where humor can be easily added are at the beginning of the presentation and at the end or at the transition between major sections of the presentation. Let me give you an example. During my popular two-day presentation skills workshop, I include a section on dealing with speaking anxiety. Here is a quote I have used as part of my introduction to this segment.

> Mark Twain said it best, "There are two types of speakers. Those that are nervous and those that are liars."

This quote always results in a little chuckle from the audience. There are many books you can use for humorous quotes. There are even websites that publish a library of quotes for all occasions.

There are also times when you can quote someone else who has used a humorous quote. Here is one such example: Steve Allen, the famous musician and past host of *The Tonight Show* said, "I do not know why they call it stage fright. Stage fright does not begin when you get up on stage; it begins the moment they ask you to get up on stage."

Closings

The end or closing of a presentation is very important. You want to end your presentation on a strong note. The closing is where you have one more opportunities to review what you presented about and then offer your audience a "call to action." Tell your audience what to do with the information you just provided them.

Following are just a few ways you can achieve a strong closing:

1. Tick off you main points verbally as you summarize them.
2. Summarize your main ideas.
3. Restate your presentations purpose.
4. Use a visual aid that includes your major points.
5. Make a direct appeal to the audience (call to action).
6. Look ahead (prediction).
7. Ask a rhetorical question.
8. Refer to your opening comments.
9. Conclude with the quote or anecdote.

I personally like to use a combination of these. Also, try to tie in your ending with your main purpose in giving the presentation. Never close a presentation by saying, "And in closing" or "And in conclusion" or even worse, "Well, I guess that's it."

Always review what you have told your audience. Tell them not only what you told them but why you told them. This can be done effectively by going back to the original agenda. Say a sentence or two about each item to remind them briefly what they have heard.

YOUR CALL TO ACTION

In Chapter 3, I discussed the importance of providing an audience a call to action. Since you have been my audience in this printed presentation, here is your call to action.

I ask each of you to review your own speaking style by using the recording techniques I talked about in this book. How many of your distracting mannerisms persist? How do you look as a presenter? Are your visual aids easy to read? How are your walking patterns? Do you make eye contact with all of your audience members? How many uhs or uhms do you use?

After every presentation you deliver, ask yourself the following questions:

1. How could I have improved this presentation?

2. What didn't I like about my last presentation?

3. What were my good points?

4. What questions did my listeners ask? (These are clues that suggest that the information may need to be presented differently.)

5. Should I revamp the presentation?

6. Do I need to review a section of this book before preparing for my next presentation?

7. While watching excellent presenters and observing their good qualities, what do I notice about their use of visuals?

Preparing a presentation is a lot of work and requires numerous hours to prepare and deliver a good, dynamic presentation. It does not have to be painful, but you do need to put in the right amount of effort. You have heard the expression "No pain, no gain." I do not feel this process needs to be painful. Yes there will be curves, bumps, detours, and delays along the way. None of these should deter you from continuing along the path to presentation excellence. You do need to make the time to do it right. My wish for you is that your journey be interesting and enriching and that you progress in making great strides toward your speaking goals. Follow the advice I have provided in this book, and your next presentation will be painless and less stressful.

Index

A

acronyms, motivational, 69—71

Allen, Steve, 24, 182—183

anxiety. *See* speaking anxiety

apologies, avoiding, 34—35

appearance, importance of, 104—105, 126, 158

ASCAP, 98

attentiveness, audience, 84—85, 136, 155

Audience

  calls to action for, 71—72, 183, 184—185

  facing when speaking to, 105, 127

  knowing and researching, 9—16, 30—31, 61, 175

  lack of concern for, 76

  monitoring reactions of, 13, 18—20

  preparing presentation setting for, 118—121

  as presentation aspect, 3, 4, 9—16

  size of, 16, 152

  surveying, 12—16

audio visual requirements, 49—50

auditory (aural) communication channels, 17

auditory (aural) learning, 109, 111—113

B

body, of presentations, 67, 69—70

body language. *See* nonverbal communication

body movement

  benefits of using, 147—148